# THE
# GRAMMAR
# COOKBOOK

# THE GRAMMAR COOKBOOK

*Bite-Sized Nuggets of
Grammatical Know-How*

**Pat Bensky**

First Edition
Published in Great Britain 2004
by
Tracker Press

© Pat Bensky

ISBN 0-9546105-0-4

www.trackerpress.com

Cover design by David Foreman
david@toastdesign.co.uk

# Contents

# Introduction

## Why should you care about your grammar?

We have two short answers to this question:

1. To make sure that people understand exactly what you mean to say.
2. So that you don't embarrass yourself or your company/organisation.

## About this book

This book isn't intended to be an English-language text book. We are not going to bog you down with the mechanics of sentence construction, dangling participles, adverbs, adjectives, past imperfect tense and so on. This book is intended for people who simply want to make sure that they avoid the most common grammatical errors in their written communications.

## How to use *The Grammar Cookbook*

We have written this book in an easy-going style that you should find enjoyable to read. We've included useful examples and a few amusing anecdotes to keep it light. It is presented in a topic-per-page style, so you can use it in any of the following ways:

1. Read a topic or two a day to gradually build up your knowledge.
2. Browse through and pick out topics that you're curious about (for example, "Should I put an apostrophe in 'its'?")
3. Use the Index to look up the answers to specific questions (for example, "Should I use 'i.e.' or 'e.g.' when giving an example?")
4. Take it on holiday and read it from beginning to end like a novel.

# Symbols

Throughout the book you will see certain symbols, which are intended to draw your attention to important features.

*The Heartbeat*

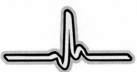

Where you see the heartbeat symbol in a topic heading, this indicates that this topic is VITAL. It isn't a question of deciding whether or not you want to follow the rule or adopt the popular usage: it is just WRONG not to follow the rule!

Over the years, many grammatical rules have been relaxed or changed due to popular usage. There has been much debate over how strict one should be in the application of these rules; sometimes, the correct usage simply appears old-fashioned compared to current popular usage, and some rules, if strictly enforced, would cause the text to appear stilted and unnatural. In many cases, it's a question of style, and you can decide for yourself whether you want to follow the recommended style or go your own way. But when you see the heartbeat symbol at the top of the page, you know that it would be wrong to ignore the advice presented on that page, and you will look foolish if you do!

*Thumbs Up and Thumbs Down*

On most topics we will give examples of the correct and incorrect usage. The "thumbs up" and "thumbs down" symbols draw your attention to the correct and incorrect usage examples:

This is an example of correct usage.

This is an example of incorrect usage.

# UK and USA Usage

In some cases, the usage differs between the UK and the USA. In such cases, we will include the Stars and Stripes and/or the Union Jack to highlight the difference.

# Thanks!

Thanks to the following people for their assistance in compiling this book:

Jo Bensky, Pauline Key-Kairis, Jeff Potter, Paul Gauthier, Florin Alexander Newmann, Roger Shuttleworth, Jo Sidebottom.

# Section 1

# *Punctuation*

*"We employ only high quality drivers."*

Hmmm. Personally, I would prefer my driver to be sober.

The way you use commas, apostrophes, hyphens, and other punctuation can change the meaning of a sentence in subtle (and sometimes not-so-subtle) ways. This section shows you how to use punctuation to ensure that your readers understand exactly what you want to say.

*"We employ only high-quality drivers."*

Oh. OK then. (See Pages 22–25 for an explanation of the use of hyphens.)

# Punctuation

## Acronyms and Initialisms

An **acronym** is a pronounceable word that is created by taking the first letters of each word of a name. Here are some examples of acronyms:

AIDS (Acquired Immune Deficiency Syndrome)
LASER (Light Amplification by Stimulated Emission of Radiation)
LASER (alternative, tongue-in-cheek version: Look at Source, Erase Retina)
PIN (Personal Identification Number)
SCUBA (Self-Contained Underwater Breathing Apparatus)
TIFF (Tagged Image File Format)

An **initialism** is what you have if you take the first letters of each word in a name and end up with something that is **not** pronounceable. Here are some examples of initialisms:

ATM (Automated Teller Machine)
EPSF (Encapsulated PostScript Format)
IBM (International Business Machines)
ISBN (International Standard Book Number)
UPC (Universal Product Code)

It's quite a common mistake to repeat the word that is represented by the last letter in an acronym or initialism, as in:

ATM machine (you're saying "Automated Teller Machine machine").
PIN number (you're saying "Personal Identification Number number").
HIV virus (you're saying "Human Immunodeficiency Virus virus").
ISBN number (you're saying "International Standard Book Number number").

Acronymns and initialisms are always in all uppercase letters.

If you are not sure about the meaning of an acronym or initialism, you can try looking it up on the Acronym Finder web site (www.acronymfinder.com).

# Punctuation

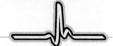

## Apostrophes—Who Needs Them?

Apostrophes are the most widely misunderstood of all punctuation marks.

**The rules are quite simple really. Apostrophes are used for three reasons:**

1. To indicate that something has been **abbreviated.**
2. To indicate that something has been **contracted**.
3. To indicate **possession** (that something belongs to somebody or something).

In this topic we will look at the first case:

### 1. Using an apostrophe to indicate that something has been abbreviated.

If you shorten a word by omitting one or more letters, you should insert an apostrophe to show that something is missing.

"**1990s**" becomes " **'90s**".
"Rock **and** roll" becomes "Rock **'n'** roll" (the "n" is surrounded by apostrophes, because two letters are missing).
"**Government**" becomes "**Gov't**".
"**cannot**" becomes "**can't**".

> *My daughter's primary school teacher taught her pupils a marvellous little saying to help them remember this: "It's as if a thief came and stole a few letters, and left a little footprint behind." It's a bit simplistic, but it works!*

**Next Topic** In the next topic we discuss the use of an apostrophe to indicate the possessive case (that something belongs to somebody).

# Punctuation

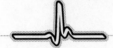

## Apostrophes—2: Contractions

**2. Using an apostrophe to show that two or more words have been contracted into one.**

When you combine two words into one to abbreviate them, the apostrophe is placed where the missing letter or letters would have been. Here are some examples:

"**it is**" becomes "**it's**"
"**we have**" becomes "**we've**"
"**they are**" becomes "**they're**"
"**is not**" becomes "**isn't**"
"**should have**" becomes "**should've**"
"**would have**" becomes "**would've**"
"**has not**" becomes "**hasn't**"

# Punctuation

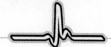

## Apostrophes—3: The Possessive Apostrophe

### 3. Using an apostrophe to show that something belongs to somebody or something.

For example:

*Mike's work is of the highest quality.*
*The managing director's decision is final.*

 John's dog bit the postman.

 Johns dog bit the postman.

Somewhat confusingly, "its" when used to refer to "something belonging to it" does NOT need an apostrophe. The reason for this is that **its**, along with **his**, **hers**, **ours**, and **theirs**, is a **possessive pronoun**. So you would not use "it's" in this case any more than you would use "hi's", because its "possessiveness" is already indicated by the fact that the word is a **possessive** pronoun.

 The dog gnawed happily on **its** bone.

 The dog gnawed happily on **it's** bone.

 Nobody makes a widget of better quality than **ours**.

 Nobody makes a widget of better quality than **our's**.

# Punctuation

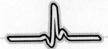

## Apostrophes—4: When NOT to Use an Apostrophe

Pay attention now—this is probably the most common punctuation mistake of all!

It is a popular misconception that whenever a word ends with an "s", there should be an apostrophe before the "s".

THIS IS NOT CORRECT!

**An apostrophe is not required when the word is a plural.**

 There are **lots** of uses for our product.

 There are **lot's** of uses for our product.

 We sell **hundreds** of these every day.

 We sell **hundred's** of these every day.

Many people are under the impression that, despite the plural rule, an apostrophe is still appropriate if the word ends with a vowel. This is not correct! Most words that end with vowels are pluralised by adding "es" (there are some exceptions: "radios", for example).

 **Tomatoes** and **potatoes** are on special offer today!

 **Tomato's** and **potato's** are on special offer today!

# Punctuation

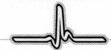

## Apostrophes—5: Possessive AND Plural

### What if the word is both possessive and plural?

In this case, the apostrophe goes **after** the "s".

> *My local supermarket has a café for the benefit of its customers. A sign above the entrance reads "Welcome to the Shopper's Café." This seems to indicate that the café is for only one shopper!*

---

 Welcome to the Shoppers' Café (multiple shoppers are welcome).

 Welcome to the Shopper's Café (only one shopper please!).

---

The difference in meaning can be very significant. Consider the following two sentences:

> *The girl's room was a mess.*
> *The girls' room was a mess*

Which one is correct? Well, it depends on how many girls inhabit the room. If the room has one inhabitant, then it is a **girl's** room. If the room has more than one inhabitant, then it's a **girls'** room.

Thanks to Jeff Potter for the following anecdote:

> *For years, I've driven by an optical shop in western Massachusetts called "Kens' Eyewear". It would drive me up the wall.*
>
> *I actually stopped in once after a co-worker told me it was otherwise a fine establishment.*
>
> *As I was waiting for my glasses, I started to say something to Ken, when I looked on the wall and saw two highfalutin ophthalmology diplomas: one for one guy named Ken, the other for another guy named Ken. As business partners, it was legitimately Kens' Eyewear.*
>
> *I told the one Ken that I was mortified that I had wasted so much fury so unfairly every time I had driven by.*
>
> *"We get hate mail" he told me.*

# Punctuation

## Apostrophes—6: Exceptions to the Rule

There had to be at least one, didn't there?

**It is acceptable to insert an apostrophe in situations where not to do so would create confusion or misunderstanding.**

A good example of this is "do's and don'ts".

Technically, the apostrophe does not belong in "do's" because it is a plural (things to do). However, "dos" could easily be confusing to the reader; what is a "dos"? Is it the Spanish word for the number two, a computer operating system, or things to do? Inserting the apostrophe makes the meaning clear.

Another example is with plurals of lowercase letters, as in "Mind your p's and q's".

**More Info** If you would like to find out more about apostrophes, the best place to look is the Apostrophe Protection Society's web site at www.apostrophe.fsnet.co.uk

# Punctuation

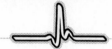

## Capital Letters—1

There seems to be a certain amount of confusion over when words should begin with a capital letter. Here are the rules:

1. Every sentence begins with a capital letter.
2. Proper nouns begin with a capital letter (a proper noun is the name of an actual person, place or event).
3. Special rules apply to headlines.

### 1. Every Sentence Begins with a Capital Letter

The first word in every sentence must begin with a capital letter. There is a good reason for this: It makes the text easy to read and comprehend.

 Here is some information. And here is some more.

 here is some information. and here is some more.

We often see words capitalised within sentences—presumably in an attempt to make them stand out or make them look important. This is incorrect, unless the words are proper nouns (see the next topic). If you want to make a word or phrase stand out, set it in bold, or italics, or underline it.

 These products are the **very best** money can buy!

 These Products are the Very Best money can buy!

### Exceptions to the Rule
An exception to this rule is in the case of headlines—see Page 11 for a discussion of this case.

Also, if part of a proper noun (a name of an actual person or place) would normally begin with a lowercase letter (for example, von, de, etc.), then it should still appear in lowercase if it appears at the beginning of a sentence.

# Punctuation

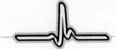

## Capital Letters—2: Proper Nouns

### 2. Proper Nouns

A proper noun is the name of a **specific** person, place, or event. A generic person, place or event is not a proper noun. For example, if you are referring to doctors in general, "doctor" should not be capitalised because it does not refer to a specific person.

 The **doctor** in charge of the operation said it had gone well.

 The **doctor** in charge (Doctor Robinson) said the operation had gone well.

 The **Doctor** in charge of the operation said it had gone well.

 The couple wanted to get married in a **cathedral**.

 The couple wanted to get married in **Westminster Cathedral**.

 The couple wanted to get married in a **Cathedral**.

**I** is **always** capitalised because it is a proper noun—it refers to a specific person: yourself.

 The employees and **I** do not agree on all points of the contract.

 The employees and **i** do not agree on all points of the contract.

# Punctuation

## Capital Letters—3: Headlines

### 3. Special Rules Apply to Headlines

The generally accepted rules for capitalisation in headlines are:

1. The first and last words are capitalised.
2. **The**, **a**, and **an** are lowercased.
3. Prepositions ("linking" words such as **through** and **with**) are lowercased, regardless of length, unless they are stressed.
4. Conjunctions ("joining" words—**and**, **but**, **for**, **or**, and **nor**) are lowercased.
5. The words **to** and **as** are lowercased.
6. Lowercase the second part of a species name or that part of a proper noun that would normally be lowercased, such as **von** or **de**.
7. All other words are capitalised.

Here are some examples:

> *An Apple a Day Keeps the Doctor Away ("An" is uppercased because it is the first word.)*
> *Old but Still Young at Heart*
> *Directors Vote for Office Relocation*
> *Directors Vote For or Against the Office Relocation (here, For is capitalised because it is stressed.)*
> *Going to the Beach*
> *James van Outenberg Appointed as Marketing Director*

Note that these rules are really just guidelines; the Grammar Police aren't going to come beating your door down if you stray away from the rules a little.

# Punctuation

## Colons

A colon looks like this: **:**
Colons are frequently confused with semicolons (which look like this **;**), but they do in fact have quite different purposes. Here is the rule for colons:

**A colon introduces an element or series of elements that illustrate or expand upon what has preceded it.**

For example:

> *The Super Gizmo is available in five colours: red, green, blue, yellow, and pink.*

> *Our service is the best: We have fully trained technicians, helpful technical support staff, and a full range of spare parts.*

> *You have two choices: Fix the problem now and know that you can rely on the computer to continue working, or leave it and wait for the hard disk to crash and destroy all your data.*

You may have noticed that in the first example, the first word following the colon was not capitalised, but in the second and third examples, it was. There is a reason for this. Here's the rule:

When a colon is used within a sentence (as in the first example), you do not capitalise the first word following the colon. But when it introduces one or more sentences (as in the second and third examples), then the first word following the colon is capitalised. If you're not sure about this, think about whether the colon could be replaced by a full stop (period, to you Americans). If it could, then the next word should be capitalised.

# Punctuation

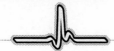

## Commas

The comma is a useful little character that can be used in a number of ways to create different effects. But its main purpose in life is to give structure to sentences—especially long ones or ones that contain a number of different thoughts. When a person comes across a comma, he knows that it signifies a slight pause or a change in the thought pattern of the sentence.

Try reading this sentence:

*We have provided a number of options from which you may choose including red green yellow and blue as well as various sizes such as small medium and large.*

It isn't very easy to read, is it? A few well-placed commas improve the sentence's readability:

*We have provided a number of options from which you may choose, including red, green, yellow and blue, as well as various sizes such as small, medium, and large.*

Commas in the wrong places can subtly change the meaning of a sentence. Consider this sentence with and without the comma:

*We offer the best things, in small packages.*
*We offer the best things in small packages*

**With** the comma, it means that our products are the best, and we supply them in small packages. **Without** the comma, it means that ours are the best things available in small packages; another supplier might have better things but in larger packages.

It isn't always easy to decide whether or not a comma should be inserted at a particular point in the sentence. Just try reading the sentence back to yourself, both with and without the comma, and see which version conveys your intended meaning most accurately. Even famous authors sometimes have trouble with this. Here's a quote that has been attributed to Oscar Wilde:

*"I was working on the proof of one of my poems all the morning, and took out a comma. In the afternoon I put it back again."*

# Punctuation

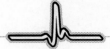

## Commas—2: Comma Splices

A **comma splice** is what you get when you use a comma to separate two sentences when you should use a full stop (period) or a semicolon.

 The word on the Teleprompter was "nuclear". The president said "nuke-ya-ler".

 The word on the Teleprompter was "nuclear"; the president said "nuke-ya-ler".

 The word on the Teleprompter was "nuclear", the president said "nuke-ya-ler".

Alternatively, you could join the two sentences together with a conjunction (one of those short thought-joining words such as **and**, **but**, **although**, **or**, **if**, and **since**).

For example:

*The word on the Teleprompter was "nuclear", **but** the president said "nuke-ya-ler".*

**Next Topic**  Subordinate Clauses

# Punctuation

## Commas—3: Subordinate Clauses

A subordinate clause can be thought of as a part of a sentence that could be taken out without making nonsense of the sentence.

Consider this example:

*She stood up, and walking quickly, went into the kitchen.*

The subordinate clause in this sentence is **walking quickly**—you could take that part out of the sentence, and it would still make sense.

So the commas should go around those two words:

*She stood up and, walking quickly, went into the kitchen.*

It makes the sentence easier to read and understand. And that, of course, is the whole point of punctuation.

# Punctuation

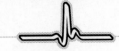

## Dashes

Dashes and hyphens are often confused—but there **is** a difference!

A dash is longer than a hyphen; exactly how much longer depends on the size of the font that is being used. In fact there are several types of dash—we will discuss the two most important ones: the **en dash** and the **em dash**.

Here is an en dash: – .
Here is an em dash: — .
As you can see, both of them are longer than a hyphen: - .

A detailed discussion of the usage of different types of dash is beyond the scope of this book, but if you follow these basic rules your results will be perfectly acceptable.

### 1. The en dash
An **en dash** (also called an **en rule** in the UK) is half the length of an **em dash** (see the next topic). Originally, it was calculated as the width of a capital N—hence its name.

*When to use an en dash*
Use an en dash in place of the word "to". For example:

> *The war lasted from 1939–1945.*
> *The Glasgow–Edinburgh train departs at 14:55.*
> *Our office hours are 9AM–5PM.*

*How to type an en dash*

On a Macintosh computer, type Alt-hyphen.
On Windows, type Alt+0150 (keep holding down the Alt key as you type the numbers, then let it go).

# Punctuation

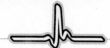

## Dashes—2: The em Dash

### 2. The em dash
An **em dash** (also called an **em rule** in the UK) is one em in length. What's an em? It is a unit of type measurement equal to the point size of the type in use. For example, if the type is set at 12 points, then an em is 12 points wide. Originally, it was calculated as the width of a capital M—hence its name.

*When to use an em dash*
Use an em dash in the following situations:
1. To separate the clauses (or thoughts) within a sentence.
2. To show hesitation within speech or to create a dramatic pause.
3. To indicate an afterthought.
4. To introduce a list.

### 1. To separate the clauses (or thoughts) within a sentence
*When you try our scrumptious Belgian chocolates—and you know you want to—you'll agree they are the best you've ever tasted.*

### 2. To show hesitation within speech or to create a dramatic pause
Use an em dash to indicate a more significant pause than a comma or semicolon.
*I—um—don't know—I just—er—found it there!*

*Mickey opened the door cautiously and saw what had sent Sara running from the room, screaming—a huge spider on the toilet seat.*

### 3. To indicate an afterthought
*Finish off your meal with one of our delicious freshly prepared desserts—if you still have room left.*

### 4. To introduce a list
You can use an em dash instead of a colon to introduce a list.
*You'll find a marvellous selection of goodies in our special Christmas hamper—wine, cakes, tinned ham, chocolate biscuits and a box of party favours.*

*How to type an em dash*
On a Macintosh, type shift-alt-hyphen. On Windows, type Alt+0151 (keep holding down the Alt key as you type the numbers, then let it go).

| | |
|---|---|
| **More Info** | If you would like more information about dashes and their use, refer to The Chicago Manual of Style or The Oxford Style Manual. |

# Punctuation

## Ellipses

A series of three dots like this: … is called an **ellipsis** (**ellipsis** is the singular of **ellipses**).

**Ellipses** are used for two reasons:

1. To indicate that one or more words are missing from the text.
2. To indicate that there might be more to come (when used at the end of a sentence).

### 1. To indicate that one or more words are missing from the text
You might use an ellipsis when you are quoting a passage from a book, letter, magazine article, etc., and you want to include only the pertinent part of the text. For example:

> *The instruction manual specifically states "… must not be used under water."*

### 2. To indicate that there might be more to come

> *I feel that we have covered all possible eventualities in our revised proposal. But you never know …*

This device is often used to add a little suspense:

> *John carefully locked all the doors and windows before he left for the night. But he didn't notice the light leaking out from under the stockroom door …*

Note that, typographically, an ellipsis is not simply three individual dots in a row: it is an actual character in its own right. Whilst three dots in a row probably look exactly the same as an ellipsis, the difference is that an ellipsis will never be broken across a line, whereas if you simply type three dots, it could happen.

*How to type an ellipsis*

On a Macintosh computer, type alt+semicolon.

On Windows, type Alt+0133 (keep holding down the Alt key as you type the numbers, then let it go).

# Punctuation

 **Exclamation Marks**

 **Exclamation Points**

The exclamation mark (point) is used to show an outcry or an emphatic comment. They should be used sparingly, and never more than one in a row.

Usually the exclamation mark is used at the end of a sentence, in which case it replaces the full stop (period).

*I can't believe you paid that much for that printer!*

**When used with quotation marks, brackets, or parentheses**
An exclamation mark should be placed inside quotation marks, brackets, or parentheses only when it is part of the quoted or parenthetical text.

In this example, the exclamation mark was part of the sales manager's comment:

*The sales manager told us "We must get rid of all these beds this week!"*

But in this example, the exclamation mark belongs to my comment, and not what Raj said:

*I couldn't believe it when Raj said "I always listen to what you say"!*

# Punctuation

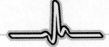

 ## Full Stops

 ## Periods

The little dot is used for two reasons:

1. To mark the end of a sentence.
2. To indicate an abbreviation.

### 1. To mark the end of a sentence

Most sentences end with a full stop (period); in fact, every sentence MUST end with a full stop or another punctuation mark such as an exclamation or question mark.

> 👍 Check out the offers on our web site. We're constantly adding new ones!
>
> 👎 Check out the offers on our web site We're constantly adding new ones!

The end of a sentence is ALWAYS followed by a space unless it is the end of the paragraph.

The next sentence must begin with a capital letter.

### Note:

Headings and subheadings do not end with a full stop. This is because they are not complete sentences—they are simply titles.

**Next Topic**  Indicating an abbreviation.

# Punctuation

## Full Stops (Periods)—2: Indicating an Abbreviation or Contraction

The question of when to use full stops in abbreviations and contractions is to some extent a style decision, with slightly different styles being prevalent in the US and the UK. We recommend the following easy-to-remember guidelines:

If the abbreviation is in all lower case or mixed case, insert full stops. For example:

| | |
|---|---|
| *i.e.* | *Thurs.* |
| *e.g.* | *Jones and Co.* |

If it's all uppercase, omit the full stops. For example:

| | |
|---|---|
| *AM* | *PO Box* |
| *CEO* | *USA* |

But don't omit them for initials:

*P. G. Wodehouse*　　*W. C. Fields*

If the abbreviation has become a commonly accepted pronounceable word, the full stop can be left off. For example:

| | |
|---|---|
| *afro* | *demo* |
| *decaf* | *mayo* |

Civil and social titles are treated differently in the US and UK:

 A full stop **is not** normally included. For example:
*Mr, Ms, Dr, Supt, Fr*

A full stop (period) **is** normally included. For example:
*Mr., Ms., Dr., Supt., Fr.*

Some typing instructors teach their students that it is acceptable to omit the full stops from all abbreviations. This is not correct—it's just a trick to increase the students' typing speed!

# Punctuation

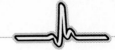

## Hyphens—1

Hyphens are used in the following circumstances:
1. To join two or more words together to avoid ambiguity.
2. To indicate that a word has been broken across two lines.
3. To link numbers.

### 1. Using a hyphen to join two words together

It is helpful to your readers to hyphenate words in situations where the meaning could otherwise be ambiguous. For example, is "a spare room heater" a heater for the spare room, or a heater that isn't currently being used? Add a hyphen in the appropriate place to clarify the meaning: "a spare-room heater" or "a spare room-heater".

How many times have you had to read a sentence two or three times to try and make sense of it? The thoughtful use of hyphens will make your sentences much clearer.

> When you hear the expression "The police searched the suspect's room with a fine tooth comb" do you wonder exactly what that means? What is a tooth comb? Who do you know that combs their teeth? It's a bit of a puzzle, isn't it? This particular phrase is so much misunderstood that we have even seen it abbreviated to "The police searched the suspect's room with a tooth comb."
> Let's try adding a well-placed hyphen:
> "The police searched the suspect's room with a fine-tooth comb."
> Now it makes sense! It's the comb that has fine teeth, not the teeth that are being combed.
> (This phrase originates from the use of a nit comb—a special comb with finely-spaced teeth used for combing nits and lice out of hair.)
> (Note: The grammatically correct version is actually "fine-toothed comb".)

Thanks to *The Dilbert Newsletter* for the following anecdote:

> In Vancouver I drove past a group of concerned parents protesting the presence of prostitutes in their neighborhood. They were carrying signs that read, "Keep our street prostitution free"!
> They were getting a lot of support from passing motorists.

To make sure that they were correctly understood, the signs should have read "Keep our street prostitution-free".

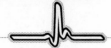

# Punctuation

## Hyphens—2: Indicating That a Word has Been Broken Across Two Lines

A hyphen is used when you need to break a word at the end of a line, because it's too long to fit.

For example:

*Our customer service is the best in the business. We are tre-*
*mendously proud of our reputation in this area.*

You must be sure to only break words between syllables.

---

 Our products are very reliable. In the unlikely event that you ex-
perience a problem, please contact the Customer Service
Department.

 Our products are very reliable. In the unlikely event that you exp-
erience a problem, please contact the Customer Service Department.

---

### Beware of rows of hyphens
You should avoid a situation in which a number of lines all end with hyphens. It looks amateurish.

### Hyphens are not surrounded by spaces.

---

 We like to think that our service is the best in the business. We are tre-
mendously proud of our reputation in this area.

 We like to think that our service is the best in the business. We are tre -
mendously proud of our reputation in this area.

---

# Punctuation

## Hyphens—3: Separating Numbers and Characters

If you need to list a series of numbers or letters, they can be linked by hyphens. For example:

*The boy dialled 9-9-9 to summon an ambulance.*

*Phone us on 800-123-1234.*

They can also be used to separate letters—for example, when you need to spell something out.

*My name is Fred Blogowizc. That's B-l-o-g-o-w-t-z-c.*

*An expert can tap out H-E-L-P in Morse code in a few seconds.*

# Punctuation

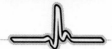

## Hyphens—4: Why Correct Hyphenation is Important

As illustrated on the previous pages, the use (or lack of) a hyphen can completely change the meaning of a sentence. Here are a few more examples to consider:

*Free range eggs*

If you don't want to have customers marching in and demanding their free eggs, it would be best to add a hyphen:

*Free-range eggs*

Here's one of my personal favourites:

*We use only high quality drivers.*

I would prefer my driver to be sober, thanks very much! Oh, did you mean that your drivers are high-quality? Then you should have said:

*We use only high-quality drivers.*

### What if more than one word is to be hyphenated?
Consider this example:

*We offer film-processing and photo-processing services.*

It sounds somewhat clumsy; you really only want to say "processing" once. In this case, you can leave out the first instance of "processing", but keep the hyphen:

*We offer film- and photo-processing services.*

### Plurals of hyphenated words
Be careful to pluralise the correct word! It's the one that is increasing.

 It was rare to find all my brothers-in-law together in one room.

 It was rare to find all my brother-in-laws together in one room.

# Punctuation

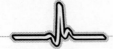

## Its and It's

Although this topic was briefly covered in the apostrophes pages, it's so important that it has earned its very own topic.

**Its** means *belonging to it*.
I**t's** is a contraction of **it is** or **it has**.

If you're ever unsure about whether to include the apostrophe or not, try applying this test:

Expand **it's** into **it is** or **it has** and then see if the sentence still makes sense. If it does, the apostrophe belongs; if not, it doesn't. For example:

"**It's** going to rain today" can safely be expanded to "**It is** going to rain today". So the apostrophe stays.

But ...

"The dog gnawed on **it's** bone" doesn't make sense if you expand it to "The dog gnawed on **it is** bone", does it? So—no apostrophe required!

---

 **It's** sale time again!

 **Its** sale time again!

---

You may well wonder why, if an apostrophe is also used to show possession, "The dog gnawed on it's bone" is wrong. The bone belongs to the dog, right? Well, yes, but **its**, in this case, is a ***possessive pronoun*** (along with **his**, **hers**, **theirs**, and **ours**). Being a possessive pronoun already signifies its "possessiveness", so you don't need to include the apostrophe.

---

 This product and all **its** associated accessories are on sale this week.

 This product and all **it's** associated accessories are on sale this week.

---

# Punctuation

## Quotation Marks (" " and ' ')

As their name suggests, quotation marks (which are also known as inverted commas) are used to indicate that something is being quoted. This could be a reference to something somebody said or a reference to, for example, some text from a book or words from a song. For example:

*The instruction manual says, "Do not try to change the film under water."*

*When you're feeling stressed out, remember the words in the song: "Don't worry—be happy"!*

They are also used to indicate when something is a little inappropriate—such as slang, made-up words, and euphemisms. For example:

*We decided to accept the sailors' offer and join them for a few "bevvies" in the pub.*

*Little Annie's grasp of the language is still developing. Today we had "gaspetti" for dinner.*

Quotation marks are often erroneously used to highlight a word.

 Breakfast served all day!

"Breakfast" served all day!

Quotation marks can either be single or double. You can choose which you prefer—but do be consistent, otherwise you'll just confuse your readers.

### Quotations within quotations
You can use a combination of single and double quotation marks to avoid confusion when you need to have a quotation within a quotation, as in this example:

*Joe said "Let's go and get a few 'bevvies' at The Old Tar".*

It's quite clear how the single and double quotation marks are paired together. The above example also illustrates why double quotation marks are generally used as the outer punctuation: because of the likelihood of an apostrophe appearing within the sentence.

# Punctuation

## Quotation Marks—2: Where to Put the Punctuation?

### 🇺🇸 US Usage

Should punctuation go inside or outside the quotation marks? There are no engraved-in-stone rules about this, but slightly different conventions are generally used in the UK and the USA.

In the USA, the most popular usage is as follows:

**Periods (full stops)** and **commas** always go *inside* the closing quotation mark, even if they seem not to belong there. For example:

*Having said "I'm really not hungry," John proceeded to devour the entire plateful.*

**Colons** and **semicolons** always go *outside* the closing quotation mark, for example:

*The waiter asked me if I was "done"; I hadn't even started!*

**Question marks, exclamation points** and **dashes** go outside the closing quotation mark unless they belong to the quoted matter, for example:

*The sales assistant asked me "Do you prefer the purple one or the pink one?"*

*Who said "Everybody deserves their fifteen minutes of fame"?*

*John started to object, saying "I wanted to explain how—" but he was cut off by the sudden arrival of the two-nosed magenta Martian.*

*Noah said, "You two and"—turning to the pair of spotted elephants— "you two as well—climb aboard now!"*

# Punctuation

## Quotation Marks—3: Where to Put the Punctuation?

### 🏴 UK Usage

The style most often used in the UK (and most other English-speaking countries, apart from the USA) is, some would say, a little more logical.

All punctuation marks go **outside** the closing quotation mark, unless they are part of the quoted matter. For example:

> *Having said, "I'm really not hungry", John proceeded to devour the entire plateful.*

> *The sales assistant asked me, "Do you prefer the purple one or the pink one?"*

> *Who said, "Everybody deserves their fifteen minutes of fame"?*

*Whether you decide to use the US or the UK style is a matter of choice. But you should pick one style or the other and stick to it, for the sake of consistency.*

# Punctuation

## Semicolons

Semicolons have two purposes in life:

1. To separate the thoughts in a sentence and create a pause.
2. To separate items in a list.

### 1. To create a pause

The purpose of punctuation is to help the reader understand exactly what you are trying to say, and to make your text easy to read. Semicolons and commas are useful devices for showing the reader where to take a little pause. As an example, try reading this sentence to yourself:

> When installing this product please make sure that the yellow hose is connected to the yellow tap the red hose is connected to the red tap and the pink hose is connected to the outlet pipe which must also be connected to the waste pipe.

Do you feel a little breathless? Not to mention, confused! Now let's try it with some thoughtfully-placed punctuation:

> When installing this product, please make sure that the yellow hose is connected to the yellow tap; the red hose is connected to the red tap; and the pink hose is connected to the outlet pipe, which must also be connected to the waste pipe.

Isn't that easier to read? Generally, a semicolon indicates a slightly longer pause than a comma.

### 2. To separate items in a list

You can also use either commas or semicolons to separate items in a list. However a semicolon should be used when one or more of the items in the list already contain commas. For example:

> We offer an extensive range of accessories for our mobile phones, including leather covers; spare batteries; replacement fascias, which are available in red, green, and purple; and in-car chargers.

# Punctuation

## Singular and Plural

You should always take care to match up the words in your sentences with regard to whether they refer to the singular or the plural. For example, use "there is" when referring to one item, and "there are" when referring to more than one item. (Remember that **here's** is a contraction of **here is**, and **there's** is a contraction of **there is**.)

 **Here are** a few suggestions.

 **Here's** a few suggestions

 **There are** hundreds of reductions in our January sale!

 **There's** hundreds of reductions in our January sale!

# Section 2

# *Word Usage*

Is it correct to say **among** or **between**? **Bought** or **brought**? In this section we've gathered a collection of frequently confused words and explained which one you should choose, and when.

# Word Usage

## a or an?

How do you know when to use **a** instead of **an**? Here are the rules:

1. Use **a** when it precedes a word that starts with a consonant (any letter other than a, e, i, o, or u).
2. Use **an** when it precedes a word that starts with a vowel (a, e, i, o, or u).

 We like to think that we offer **an** unbeatable service.

 We like to think that we offer **a** unbeatable service.

### Exception:
If a word starts with the letter u (a vowel) that sounds like a consonant, use **a** instead of **an**. For example:

*We like to think that we offer a unique service.*

### What about initialisms?
This can be a little bit tricky! Think about how the initialism will actually be pronounced. For example, "http" is pronounced "aich-tee-tee-pee", so you would refer to **an** http address.

## Words that begin with "h"
A popular misconception is that it is correct to say **an** instead of **a** with all words that begin with the letter "h". The rule is that "an" should be used only when the "h" is **normally** silent—for example *an heir* or *an honest face*. This misconception undoubtedly arose because the word *hotel* is often pronounced *'otel* (because it is a French word, and the French do not pronounce the letter *h*), so it is correct to say **an 'otel**.

 Rosemary is **a** herb that's great with lamb.

 Rosemary is **an** 'erb that's great with lamb.

# Word Usage

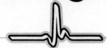

## ain't

This word is slang. It should **never, ever**, be used in formal writing.

 We **don't have** any more blue widgets in stock.

 We **ain't got** any more blue widgets in stock.

 I **don't have** any grades lower than a C.

 I **ain't got** any grades lower than a C.

The only time it is acceptable to allow this corruption of the language to make contact with paper is when quoting somebody. For example:

*The suspect continued to deny his involvement in the crime. "I ain't even been to Chicago!" he insisted.*

# Word Usage

## alot or a lot?

There is no such word as **alot**: it's two separate words.

 We put **a lot** of research into our new product.

 We put **alot** of research into our new product.

Or do you mean **allot**?

**Allot** means to parcel out, assign, or apportion.

 Each speaker will be **allotted** ten minutes for his presentation.

 Each speaker will be **alotted** ten minutes for his presentation.

# Word Usage

## among or amongst?

**Amongst** means exactly the same as **among**, and most style guides discourage its use; it is not a different word, but simply a little corruption. Why clutter up your sentence with unnecessary letters?

 Please discuss this quietly **among** yourselves.

 Please discuss this quietly **amongst** yourselves.

# Word Usage

## among or between?

**Among** is used when the choice is from more than two options; **between** is used when there are only two options from which to choose.

 You must choose **among** these six candidates.

 You must choose **between** these six candidates.

 You must choose **between** these two candidates.

 You must choose **among** these two candidates.

### Exception to the rule

It's acceptable to use **between** when referring to multiple options if multiple one-to-one relationships are understood from the context. For example, "*The purpose of this directive is to stimulate trade between Chamber members.*" Here, it is implied that the trade occurs between one member and another member.

# Word Usage

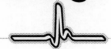

## anymore or any more?

**anymore**

 **Anymore** means at the present time, any longer, or from now on.

 We do not make purple widgets **anymore**.

 We do not make purple widgets **any more**.

 **Anymore** is not normally considered an actual word in UK English.

**any more**

**Any more** means anything or something additional or further.

 We do not have **any more** purple widgets in stock.

 We do not have **anymore** purple widgets in stock.

# Word Usage

## anyway or any way?

**Anyway** means *in any case*, *at least*, *nevertheless*, or *regardless*.

 The rain was chucking down, but we went out **anyway**.

 The rain was chucking down, but we went out **any way**.

**Any way** means *some method of doing something*.

 Is there **any way** we can improve our service?

 Is there **anyway** we can improve our service?

# Word Usage

## assume or presume?

Both of these words can mean to take for granted, or to suppose. Generally, in the interest of clarity, it's recommended that you use **presume** in this case.

 I **presume** that you possess a valid driver's licence.

 I **assume** that you possess a valid driver's licence.

However, **assume** can also have different meanings:

1. To take upon oneself: For example, you may assume responsibility when you accept a higher position at work, or you may assume someone else's debts.
2. To undertake the duties of an office: For example, "Bill assumed the presidency".
3. To take on; adopt: "The god assumes a human form".
4. To put on; don: "The magician assumed a velvet robe".
5. To affect the appearance or possession of; feign: "The actor assumed the appearance of the vice president".
6. To take over without justification; seize: "The dictator assumed control of the country while it was in chaos following the death of the president".

# Word Usage

## beside or besides?

**Beside** means *next to*.

**Besides** means *in addition to*.

 I am an accomplished guitarist and a great cook **besides**.

 I am an accomplished guitarist and a great cook **beside**.

 We were **beside** ourselves with laughter.

 We were **besides** ourselves with laughter.

# Word Usage

## borrow or lend?

These two words complement each other: the person who is parting with something is doing the **lending**, and the person who is on the receiving end is doing the **borrowing**.

 May I **borrow** your pen for a minute?

 I will gladly **lend** you my pen.

 May I **lend** your pen for a minute?

# Word Usage

## bought or brought?

**Bought** is the past tense of **buy**
**Brought** is the past tense of **bring**

 I **bought** a new TV at the supermarket today.

 I **brought** a new TV at the supermarket today.

 I've **brought** a bottle of wine with me.

 I've **bought** a bottle of wine with me.

# Word Usage

## careening or careering?

**Careen** means to tilt to one side, and more specifically, in nautical terms, to turn a ship onto its side for the purpose of cleaning or repairing it.

**Career** means to rush wildly, move or run fast.

The two words are easily mixed up, perhaps because the "modern" meaning of **career** leads us to think that it can't mean rushing around wildly—and so, not being entirely sure of the meaning of the very similar word, **careen**, we think that that's the word to use in this context.

 The car **careered** wildly down the road, completely out of control.

 The car **careened** wildly down the road, completely out of control.

# Word Usage

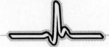

## comprises or comprised of?

**Comprises** means *consists of* or *is made up of*. Since the meaning of the word already includes "of", it is incorrect to say comprises of—if you do this, it's like saying "consists of of".

 The kit **comprises** a camera, battery, and a roll of film.

 The kit **comprises of** a camera, battery, and a roll of film.

# Word Usage

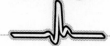

## could care less

If you think about it, this phrase doesn't really make sense! What you probably mean is "... **_couldn't_** care less ..."

If you say "I **could** care less what the boss thinks—I'm gong to give you the discount anyway!" you are saying that you DO care what the boss thinks, which makes the sentence sound a bit silly. However, if you say "I **couldn't** care less what the boss thinks ...", you're telling the customer that you DON'T care whether the boss approves or not—he's going to get his discount anyway.

 I **couldn't care less** how you feel about that.

 I **could care less** how you feel about that.

# Word Usage

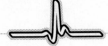

## could of

What you actually mean to say is "could have"; "could of" is nonsense! It's easy to see where the misunderstanding has come from: we frequently abbreviate **could have** to **could've**, which sounds very much like **could of**.

 I **could have** just died when he told me he was already married.

 I **could've** just died when he told me he was already married.

 I **could of** just died when he told me he was already married.

# Word Usage

---

## data or datum?

**Data** is the plural form of **datum**: one piece of information is a **datum**, and more than one piece of information is **data**.

However, the use of **data** to refer to any number of pieces of information has become so accepted in modern usage that it is no longer considered an egregious error to use it in sentences such as "This data is incorrect!" when referring to only one piece of information.

In fact it could be argued that **data** is a collective noun and so it is perfectly correct to use it as either a singular or a plural word, depending on the context (see the Points of Grammar section for an explanation of what a collective noun is).

So the simple answer is: it's safe to use **data** no matter how many pieces of information you're talking about, unless you want to specifically make a point that you are referring to one piece of information. So the following are all acceptable:

*This data is incorrect!* (Could be one or more pieces of data.)

*These data are incorrect!* (More than one piece of data.)

*This datum is incorrect!* (One piece of data.)

# Word Usage

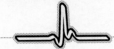

## date or day?

**Date** means a specific day in a specific month in a specific year.

**Day** means a 24-hour period from midnight to midnight.

 The same thing happened on this **day** last year.

 The same thing happened on this **date** last year.

"This date" can only exist once as it refers to a specific day, month, and year—e.g., January 1st. 2004—so the same date could not have existed last year!

# Word Usage

## different from, different than or different to?

Generally, **different than** is frowned upon by grammatical purists, with **different from** being the preferred form.

 The British are also fond of the form **different to**, and this is quite acceptable, although it may sound a little weird to people from other English-speaking countries.

In some circumstances, though, **different from** just doesn't sound right. Would you say "The town is **different from** it was twenty years ago" or "The town is **different than** it was twenty years ago"? (Technically it would be correct to change the sentence around a little and say "The town is **different from** how it was twenty years ago.")

Similarly, consider this sentence: "The female witness described the scene **differently than** the male one did."

Our advice, then, is to use **different from** (or **different to**, if you're English) unless it sounds awkward, in which case **different than** would probably sound right.

# Word Usage

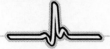

## everyday or every day?

**Everyday** means *appropriate for ordinary days or routine occasions*, or *commonplace or ordinary*.

**Every day** means *something that happens each day*.

 We have different special offers **every day**.

 We have different special offers **everyday**.

 Our suits are for special occasions—not **everyday** use.

 Our suits are for special occasions—not **every day** use.

# Word Usage

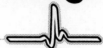

## everytime

This is not a word! What you probably mean to say is **every time**.

---

 **Every time** you contact our call centre, we will do our best to help you.

 **Everytime** you contact our call centre, we will do our best to help you.

---

# Word Usage

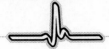

### expresso

There's no such thing as **expresso**! Perhaps what you mean is **espresso** (strong coffee). This word is of Italian origin, and perhaps it looks a little odd in English, whereas **expresso** appears to be more meaningful. But it isn't!

# Word Usage

## fewer or less?

You should use **fewer** when referring to things that can be counted (such as people, cans of beans, pets, etc.) and **less** when referring to amounts or mass nouns (uncountable things) such as water, salt, or dirt.

 Use this checkout if you have **fewer than** 10 items.

 There's **less** hot air in the little balloon than the big one.

 Use this checkout if you have **less than** 10 items.

# Word Usage

## flammable or inflammable?

These two words both mean the same thing: capable of being set on fire.

The original word was **inflammable**, however, this caused much dangerous confusion as many people thought that the "in" prefix meant "not"—an easy mistake to make, when you think of an example such as **inappropriate**, which means **not appropriate**.

Our advice is to use **flammable**, as then there is no ambiguity, and if you want to say that something is not flammable, say **non-flammable** (since non-inflammable is likely to cause even more confusion).

# Word Usage

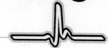

## free gift

Do you normally charge for your gifts?

 **A gift** with every purchase!

 **Free gift** with every purchase!

Admittedly, the correct version doesn't sound as enticing. But you could jazz it up a little by saying something like "A fantastic gift with every purchase!"

# Word Usage

## fullest

Be careful how you use this word! It should be used only when comparing things, as in "the plastic jug is the **fullest** one", (meaning: the plastic jug is **more full** than the the other ones), and not when referring to one item being full.

 We will prosecute shoplifters to the **full** extent of the law.

 We will prosecute shoplifters to the **fullest** extent of the law.

# Word Usage

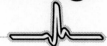

## gourmand or gourmet?

A **gourmand** is a person who greedily devours his food; a glutton.

A **gourmet**, on the other hand, is a connoisseur of good food and wines.

 Sebastian likes to think of himself as something of a **gourmet** and refuses to eat at places like Freda's Greasy Spoon.

 Sebastian is something of a **gourmand** and he'll eat just about anywhere—even places like Freda's Greasy Spoon.

 Sebastian likes to think of himself as something of a **gourmand** and refuses to eat at places like Freda's Greasy Spoon.

# Word Usage

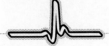

## hanged or hung?

**Hanged** is used only when referring to the hanging of a person by the neck with the intention of killing him or her.

In all other cases, **hung** is the past tense of **hang**.

 The murderer is going to be **hanged** at dawn.

 The murderer is going to be **hung** at dawn.

 We **hung** your picture on the wall.

 We **hanged** your picture on the wall.

### What about "Hung, drawn, and quartered", then? Shouldn't it be "Hanged, drawn and quartered"?

No, and this is why: "Hanged" is used when a person is hung by the neck with the intention of causing death. Being hung, drawn, and quartered is a rather different, very grisly, way to die: the person is not intended to die from the hanging but instead—slowly, painfully, and with a great deal of mess—by being slit open so that his guts spill out, and then chopped up into quarters.

# Word Usage

## his, hers, or their?

The trick here is to make sure that you match up singular and plural correctly. **His** or **hers** refers to one person, whereas **their** refers to more than one person.

 No one will change **his or her** opinion of the evil dictator.

 No one will change **their** opinion of the evil dictator.

**No one** is singular, but **their** is plural.

But in practical use, this can become rather unwieldy, and for this reason it is generally not considered a major error to use **their** when referring to people who might be male or female.

One solution is to change the sentence around a little; pluralizing is a good solution. For example, you could say "People will not change **their** opinion of the evil dictator".

# Word Usage

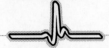

## historic or historical?

**Historic** means something momentous that happened in the past.

**Historical** refers more generally to anything that happened in the past.

 The day that World War II ended was a **historic** occasion.

The day that World War II ended was a **historical** occasion.

Be careful not to confuse **historical** with mythical! **Historical** is real; mythical is the stuff of stories and legends.

# Word Usage

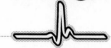

## home in or hone in?

To **home in** on something means to move towards or zoom in on it.

A **hone** is a whetstone, or other type of stone, used for sharpening things (especially razors), and **to hone** is a verb (a "doing" word) meaning to sharpen something on a hone.

So if you say that you are "honing in on the solution to the problem", you're implying that are sharpening the problem! That's probably not what you intend to say.

 We easily found the stag by **homing in** on his radio tag.

 We easily found the stag by **honing in** on his radio tag.

# Word Usage

## hopefully

This word is popularly used to mean *I hope* or *it is to be hoped*, but in fact that isn't what it actually means. The true meaning is *in a hopeful manner*.

 **I hope** that we will fulfill all outstanding orders by Friday.

 **It is to be hoped** that we will fulfill all outstanding orders by Friday.

 The dog stared **hopefully** at the cookie jar.

 **Hopefully**, we will fulfill all outstanding orders by Friday.

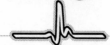

## hyper- or hypo-?

If you have a **hyper**-active child, you probably don't need reminding that **hyper** means excessive, or more than usual, whereas **hypo** means exactly the opposite: defective, inadequate, or under.

# Word Usage

## I or me?

Should you say "My partners and **me** have decided to make you an offer" or "My partners and **I** have decided to make you an offer"? To figure out the solution to this puzzle, simply split the sentence into two:

*My partners have decided to make you an offer.*
and
*I have decided to make you an offer.*

It would clearly be wrong to say

*Me have decided to make you an offer.*

So the correct answer is "My partners and **I** have decided to make you an offer".

---

 Please accept this gift from my partners and **me**.

 Please accept this gift from my partners and **I**.

---

**Also See** Also see the entry for **myself**.

# Word Usage

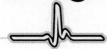

## i.e. or e.g.?

These two abbreviations are often confused, but there is an important difference in their meanings. They are both short for Latin expressions:

**i.e.** is an abbreviation for the Latin *id est*, which means *that is*.

**e.g.** is an abbreviation for the Latin *exempli gratia*, which means *for example*.

So when you are referring to something specific, you should use **i.e.**, and when you are giving an example, use **e.g.**

"The deadline for this project is in two days—**i.e.**, on Thursday"—the reference is to a specific day: "… **that is**, on Thursday".

"Please bring something to share to the picnic—**e.g.**, some of your famous potato salad"—the reference is to an example: "… **for example**, some of your famous potato salad".

 Both **i.e.** and **e.g.** are usually followed by a comma.

 The US style is not to follow **i.e.** and **e.g.** with a comma, to avoid the possibility of double punctuation.

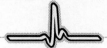

# Word Usage

## incase

This is another of those non-words! It's actually two words: **in case**.

 Let's leave early **in case** the traffic is bad.

 Let's leave early **incase** the traffic is bad.

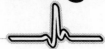

# Word Usage

## index, indexes, indice, or indices?

**Index** is singular, and **indexes** or **indices** (pronounced *in-de-sees*) are plural.

**Indice** is not an actual word at all; it's a misguided attempt to turn **indices** into a singular form.

 It's hot out there today, with a heat **index** approaching 100.

 It's hot out there today, with a heat **indice** approaching 100.

# Word Usage

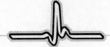

## irregardless or regardless?

**Regardless** means *without regard to*, so if you say **irregardless**, you're saying *without without regard to*—a double negative!

---

 **Regardless** of the consequences, I'm going to have another drink.

 **Irregardless** of the consequences, I'm going to have another drink.

---

**Irrespective** is a synonym (a similar-meaning word) for **regardless**, and it's likely that the confusion over **irregardless** was born out of a fusing together of the two words.

# Word Usage

## lay or lie?

To **lay** means to put—for example:

*Lay that plate down on the table over there.*

To **lie** means either to rest or to say something that isn't true. For example:

*Lie down on your stomach and lace your fingers behind your neck.*

*Do not tell me the parakeet attacked you first. That is a **lie**.*

 I'm just going to **lie** down and rest for a few minutes.

 I'm just going to **lay** down and rest for a few minutes.

# Word Usage

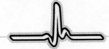

## light or lite?

**Light** means:
1. Not dark.
2. Not heavy.

**Lite** is not a real word! It is a marketing-speak word that was invented for use in situations where a company wants to imply that its product is light in fat, calories, tar, alcohol, etc., but cannot actually call it "light" because it isn't.

"**Lite** beer" might be *relatively* low in alcohol, compared to the regular version of the same brand, but it isn't truly low alcohol, so it cannot legally be called "**Light** beer". But **lite** sounds like **light**, giving a misleading impression that the product is **light**.

It could be argued that **lite** is an acceptable new word—in which case its meaning would be defined as something like: *implying that a product has a low content of some harmful substance, when in fact it does not.*

We have two problems with this:

1. It is very misleading.
2. It encourages people to believe that **lite** is the correct, or alternative, spelling for **light**. It isn't!

---

 Please switch off the **light** when you leave.

 Please switch off the **lite** when you leave.

---

# Word Usage

## literally

**Literally** means not figurative or metaphorical—in other words, it is exactly what it says it is.

 He played a solo that had the audience riveted to their seats.

 He played a solo that had the audience **literally** riveted to their seats. (The screams could be heard for miles ...)

# Word Usage

## login or log in?

**Log in** is a verb (a "doing word") meaning to enter a password or access code to gain access to something.

**Login** is a noun (a "thing" word) referring to an actual phrase or code word. The two should not be mixed up.

 Please **log in** to the database by entering your user name and password.

 Please **login** to the database by entering your user name and password.

 Your **login** code is "sunshine".

 Your **log in** code is "sunshine".

# Word Usage

## luxuriant or luxurious?

**Luxuriant** means over-abundant or profuse.

**Luxurious** means sumptuous, indulgent, or rich.

 We frolicked in the **luxuriantly** deep, green, sweet-smelling meadow.

 We frolicked in the **luxuriously** deep, green, sweet-smelling meadow.

 Our executive jet is very **luxurious**.

 Our executive jet is very **luxuriant**.

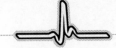

# Word Usage

### may or can?

**May** refers to being *allowed* to do something; **can** refers to being *able* to do something.

Consider the following example:

*Dad, can I use the car tonight?*

Dad might well reply, "Yes, you can, but you may not!"—meaning that you are perfectly *able* to use the car, but you're not *allowed* to.

 **May I** please have the salt?

 **Can I** please have the salt?

 **May I** borrow the car tonight?

 **Can I** borrow the car tonight?

 How **can** I help you? ("How am I **able** to help you?")

 **May** I help you? ("Am I **allowed** to help you—do you want me to?")

 How **may** I help you? (You're saying "How am I **allowed** to help you?")

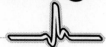

# Word Usage

## mis- or miss-?

Preceding a word with **mis-** means doing it the wrong way. For example: "mis-typing."

**Miss** means:
1. An unmarried woman or a girl.
2. The opposite of *hit*.

 The error was a result of a **mis**-interpretation of my instructions.

 The error was a result of a **miss**-interpretation of my instructions.

# Word Usage

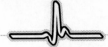

## most

It's an error to use the word **most** with an absolute—as in, for example, **most unique**. Something is either unique or it isn't—it can't be partially unique or more unique than something else.

 Our products are unique.

 Our products are the **most** unique on the market.

Sometimes **most** is mistakenly used when **almost** would be the correct choice.

 **Almost** every one of our pupils gains his or her high school diploma.

 **Most** of our pupils gain their high school diplomas.

 **Most every** one of our pupils gains his or her high school diploma.

# Word Usage

## myself

This word can be used for two reasons:

1. To show that you are doing something to yourself

   *I almost killed **myself** riding that motorcycle.*

2. To emphasise a point

   *I'll revise the proposal **myself**.*

It should not be used instead of **me** or **I**!

 For more information, please contact Dick, Jane, or **me**.

 For more information, please contact Dick, Jane, or **myself**.

 **Myself**, I prefer the blue logo to the green one.

 **Me**, I prefer the blue logo to the green one.

**Also See**

Also see the topic for I or me

# Word Usage

## nb

This is an abbreviation of the Latin *nota bene*, meaning *note well*, or *take note*.

Here is an example (from an actual instruction booklet):

> *To change the film, slide the locking catch upwards and open the back of the camera.*
> **NB**: *do not change the film under water.*

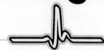

# Word Usage

## nextday

**Nextday** is not a word.

If you are tempted to use this, what you probably should be using is "next-day."

 We offer **next-day** service on all in-stock items.

 We offer **nextday** service on all in-stock items.

# Word Usage

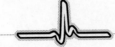

### nite

**Nite** IS NOT A WORD!

The correct spelling is **night**.

There is no plausible excuse for mis-spelling this word, and you will certainly look foolish if you do.

# Word Usage

## only

Take care with the positioning of this word within your sentences! It should go next to the word that it is modifying.

Consider the following sentence: "I **only** have five dollars". By putting the **only** with I, you're implying that you are the only person to have five dollars, when what you really mean is that five dollars is all the money you have.

 I have **only** five dollars.

 I **only** have five dollars.

# Word Usage

## oral or verbal?

**Oral** means *by mouth*.

**Verbal** means *in words*.

 I am giving you an **oral** warning.

 I am giving you a **verbal** warning.

# Word Usage

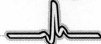

## premise or premises?

A **premise** is a proposition stated or assumed for the sake of argument, with **premises** being the plural form (also sometimes spelled **premiss**).

**Premises** can also mean a building—usually, a place of business. It's a common mistake to use **premise** instead of **premises** when referring to a place of business. It's an easy mistake to make; you might think that, since you have only one building, it's a **premise** rather than **premises**. But that would be wrong!

 All work is performed on the **premises**.

 All work is performed on **premise**.

However, it would be correct to say something like "All work is performed on the **premise** that you want the problem fixed". But that's quite a different meaning.

# Word Usage

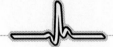

## prevaricate or procrastinate?

**Prevaricate** means to tell a lie or to avoid telling the truth, or coming to the point.

**Procrastinate** means to put something off, when it should be done immediately.

Politicians, for example, are often known to both prevaricate and procrastinate—but be sure to accuse them of the appropriate misdemeanour!

 The senator **prevaricated**, and would not give us a straight answer.

 The senator **procrastinated**, and would not give us a straight answer.

 The senator **procrastinated**, saying that he would have an answer tomorrow.

 The senator **prevaricated**, saying that he would have an answer tomorrow.

# Word Usage

## provided or providing?

Use **provided** when something has to happen before something else can happen.

 We will refund your purchase **provided** that you return the goods to us.

 We will refund your purchase **providing** that you return the goods to us.

# Word Usage

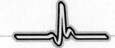

## regretful or regrettable?

If you are full of regret, then you are **regretful**. If something that is to be regretted has occurred, that is **regrettable**.

 It was a **regrettable** accident that cost us a lot of money.

 It was a **regretful** accident that cost us a lot of money.

# Word Usage

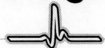

## Scotch, Scot, or Scottish?

Better get this right if you're planning a trip to Scotland!

**Scotch** means of or pertaining to Scotland, and is usually used to refer to objects (such as Scotch whisky, Scotch eggs, Scotch mist, and Scotch broth). It is generally interchangeable with **Scottish** (Scottish terrier, Scottish kilt), but shouldn't be used to refer to a person from Scotland (a **Scot**), as this is likely to cause offence.

 We just got a **Scottish terrier** puppy!.

 The **Scots** are famous for their New Year's Eve parties.

 Dad is partial to a shot of **Scotch whisky** before dinner.

 The **Scotch** people are famous for their New Year's Eve parties.

# Word Usage

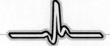

## setup or set up?

A **setup** is a noun (a "thing" word) referring to the way things are organised or arranged.

**Set up** is a verb (a "doing" word) referring to the act of organising something.

 Go ahead and get yourself **set up** in the meeting room.

 Go ahead and get yourself **setup** in the meeting room.

 You've got a pretty glamorous **setup** here!

 You've got a pretty glamorous **set up** here!

# Word Usage

## shall or will?

It's grammatically correct to use **shall** with "I" or "we", and **will** with he, she, it, they, and you.

 We **shall** endeavour to deliver the goods to you within two days.

 We **will** endeavour to deliver the goods to you within two days.

 It **will** not be possible to complete this order before Christmas.

 It **shall** not be possible to complete this order before Christmas.

 The exact meaning of the original word is something we **shall** never know.

 The exact meaning of the original word is something we **will** never know.

However, in current popular usage, **will** is frequently used in all cases, and this is acceptable to many people.

### Exception to the rule

When **will** or **shall** are being used for emphasis, the rule is reversed!

 You **shall** go to the ball!

 I **will** get a raise at my next salary review!

# Word Usage

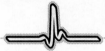

## should of

Like **could of**, this is a rather serious grammatical error! The correct phrase is **should have**. It's an easy mistake to make: **should have** is frequently abbreviated to **should've**, which sounds very much like **should of**.

 You **should have** been here when the boss found those empty gin bottles!

 You **should've** been here when the boss found those empty gin bottles!

 You **should of** been here when the boss found those empty gin bottles!

# Word Usage

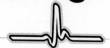

## than or then?

**Than** is a conjunction (a "joining" word) that is used:
1. To make a comparison—e.g., "I am a better athlete **than** you."
2. To introduce a difference—e.g., "I feel differently about this matter **than** you do."

**Then** means:
1. At that time—e.g., "Back **then**, I was quite naive."
2. The next thing—e.g., "We had some pizza, and **then** we went to the movies."
3. In that event—e.g., "If the meeting runs on, **then** we'll order in some sandwiches."
4. As a consequence—e.g., "The argument, **then**, is settled."

 Enter your name into the box, **then** click on the Submit button.

 Enter your name into the box, **than** click on the Submit button.

 If you knew it was malfunctioning, **then** why did you use it?

 If you knew it was malfunctioning, **than** why did you use it?

 I'd be more **than** willing to host the next party.

 I'd be more **then** willing to host the next party.

# Word Usage

## that, which or who?

In modern popular usage, **that** and **which** are generally interchangeable. Strictly speaking, though, they should be distinguished in the following way:

**That** is used restrictively to narrow a category or identify a particular thing that is being talked about.

 The item **that** is in your pocket has not been paid for.

 The item **which** is in your pocket has not been paid for.

**Which** is used non-restrictively: not to narrow a class or identify a particular item but to add something about an item already identified.

One way to distinguish them is that a **that** clause should never be preceded by a comma because it is necessary to the meaning of the sentence, whereas a **which** clause can—and should—be separated from the rest of the sentence by commas, because it could be dropped without the sentence losing meaning.

 We have a number of different products, **which** are available in various sizes, to solve your storage problems.

 We have a number of different products **that** are available in various sizes to solve your storage problems.

However, when referring to humans, you should always use **who**.

 I know a woman **who** has nine children.

 I know a woman **that** has nine children.

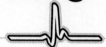

## theirselves

There is no such word as **theirselves**. The correct word is **themselves**.

 I have asked the service engineers to correct it **themselves**.

 I have asked the service engineers to correct it **theirselves**.

# Word Usage

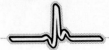

## thru

We owe no thanks at all to fast-food restaurants for this horrible and pointless corruptive abbreviation of the word **through**! We usually abbreviate words to make them shorter in speech; since **through** sounds exactly the same as **thru**, there is no point in abbreviating it.

The only possible excuse could be in the event that the writer is desperately short of space (as could, admittedly, be the case in the sign for the Drive-Through Window). In that event, the correct abbreviation is **thru'**. (Remember, an apostrophe is used to indicate that one or more letters are missing.)

There is no excuse for using **thru** in any other situation, and you will certainly look foolish if you use it in your business or formal writing.

# Word Usage

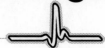

## unique

The word **unique** means *the only one of its kind*. Therefore, one thing cannot be more unique than another!

 Our widgets are **unique**—there is nothing else like them on the market.

 Our widgets are the most **unique** product on the market.

# Word Usage

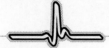

## unthaw

**Unthaw** is not a word!

**Thaw** means to un-freeze. So if you say **unthaw**, you're saying un-un-freeze, which doesn't really make a lot of sense! So just say **thaw**.

---

 The quickest way to **thaw** a frozen chicken is to immerse it in cold water.

 The quickest way to **unthaw** a frozen chicken is to immerse it in cold water.

---

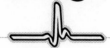

# Word Usage

## upto or up to?

**Upto** is not a word! What you mean to say is **up to**.

When you say **up to**, you're placing a limit on whatever it is you are referring to. So it doesn't make sense to follow it by offering an extension.

 SALE! Save **up to** 50%!

 SALE! Save 50% or more!

 SALE! Save **up to** 50% or more!

# Word Usage

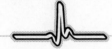

## use to

We suspect that what you actually mean to say is **used to**.

 Over the years I've simply grown **used to** it.

 Over the years I've simply grown **use to** it.

 I **used to** make lots of grammatical errors, but now I've got this book.

 I **use to** make lots of grammatical errors, but now I've got this book.

# Word Usage

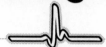

## whereas or whereby

**Whereas** means:
1. It being the fact.
2. While at the same time.
3. While on the contrary.

**Whereby** means:
1. In accordance with which.
2. By or through which.

For example: "Education is a method **whereby** people learn new things".

So you would use **whereas** when you want to show an alternative idea, and **whereby** when you want to show that something is in response to something else.

---

 I like the blue car, **whereas** my husband prefers the red one.

 I like the blue car, **whereby** my husband prefers the red one.

---

# Word Usage

## which or what?

These are used when asking a question. You should use **which** when you are asking for a choice to be made from a specific set of options, and **what** when asking for a choice to be made from an unknown number of options.

 **Which** would you prefer—the blue one or the red one?

 **What** is your name?

 **What** would you prefer—the blue one or the red one?

# Word Usage

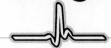

## who or whom?

This one is rather tricky to explain without getting at least a little bit technical.

If you're content with a quick and easy way to decide which to use, try this:

> *If you can replace the word with* I, he, she *or* they *then it is the subject of the sentence and you should use* **who**. *If you can replace the word with* me, him, her, us *or* them *it is the object and you should use* **whom**.

For example:
>To **whom** it may concern. (To him or her that it might concern.)
>For **whom** the bell tolls. (For him or her that the bell tolls.)
>
>**Who** has the key to the stationery cupboard? (Does he or she have the key to the stationery cupboard?)
>I was the one **who** wrote that letter. (I wrote that letter.)

If your curiosity will not be satiated with that simple solution, here's the technical explanation:

**Who** is used for a grammatical subject, where a nominative pronoun such as I or he would be appropriate, and **whom** is used as the object of a verb or preposition.

# Section 3

# *Confusables*

*"This red wine compliments the roast beef perfectly."*

Wow! Talking wine!

We're easily confused by words that look or sound the same or very similar, but have completely different meanings. In this section we look at the most frequently-confused words—the confusables.

*"This red wine complements the roast beef perfectly."*

Oh. Well, that's a different matter.

(See Page 127 for an explanation.)

# Confusables

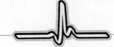

## accede/exceed

**Accede** means:
1. To give consent, usually under duress.
2. To rise into a position of power.

**Exceed** means to extend beyond or surpass.

 The prince **acceded** to the throne after his father, the king, died.

 The prince **exceeded** to the throne after his father, the king, died.

 You've **exceeded** your authority by firing the new waiter.

 You've **acceded** your authority by firing the new waiter.

# Confusables

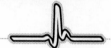

## accept/except

**Accept** means:
1. To receive something (usually gladly).
2. To admit into a group or organisation.
3. To endure with patience or resignation (e.g., **accept** one's fate).
4. To answer in the affirmative (e.g., **accept** an invitation).
5. To be able to hold something applied or inserted (e.g., the full jug will not **accept** any more water).

**Except** means:
1. If not for the fact that; only (e.g., "I would gladly hire you, **except** that you don't have a clean driver's licence").
2. Otherwise (e.g., "The prisoner didn't say a word **except** to ask for his lawyer").
3. Unless (e.g., "Don't leave the room **except** to go to the bathroom").
4. To leave out or exclude (e.g., "Admission is charged for adults, but children and pensioners are **excepted**").
5. To object to something (e.g., "The lawyer took **exception** to the judge's ruling").

 I can't **accept** that excuse for your tardiness.

 I can't **except** that excuse for your tardiness.

# Confusables

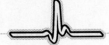

## adverse/averse

**Adverse** means unfavourable.

**Averse** means opposed to or against.

 I'm not **averse** to a little drink once in a while.

 I'm not **adverse** to a little drink once in a while.

# Confusables

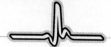

## advice/advise

**Advice** is a noun (a "thing" word) that means recommendation.

**Advise** means the same thing, except that it's a verb (a "doing" word). So, you might give some advice, but you would advise somebody.

 I'll give you some **advice**.

 I'll give you some **advise**.

 I am here to **advise** you on the correct use of the new equipment.

 I am here to **advice** you on the correct use of the new equipment.

# Confusables

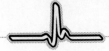

## affect/effect

**Affect** means:
1. To have an impact on.
2. To put on or pretend.

**Effect** means:
1. To bring about (e.g., to **effect** a change).
2. A consequence or result (e.g., "His comment had the **effect** of making the secretary burst into an uncontrollable fit of laughter").
3. Belongings (e.g., personal **effects**).

 That did not have the desired **effect**.

 Wally's illness had a big **effect** on his life.

 That did not have the desired **affect**.

# Confusables

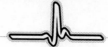

## aid/aide

**Aid** is a verb (a "doing" word) that means giving assistance or a noun (a "thing" word) meaning a piece of equipment or implement that assists in the performance of a task.

**Aide** is a noun referring to a person who provides help or assistance.

 Corporal Klinger is the Major's new **aide**.

 Corporal Klinger is the Major's new **aid**.

 I am here to **aid** you in any way I can.

 I am here to **aide** you in any way I can.

# Confusables

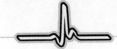

## altar/alter

An **altar** is a structure before which religious ceremonies are conducted, or sacrifices made.

To **alter** means to change in some way.

 Jim chose not to **alter** his appearance for the job interview.

 Jim chose not to **altar** his appearance for the job interview.

 We knelt before the **altar** and gave thanks for the great harvest.

 We knelt before the **alter** and gave thanks for the great harvest.

# Confusables

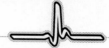

## aural/oral

**Aural** refers to the ear, whereas **oral** refers to the mouth.

 Chocolate gives me great **oral** satisfaction.

 Pinching my earlobe gives me some **aural** satisfaction, whilst hearing a good poem gives me great auditory satisfaction..

 Chocolate gives me great **aural** satisfaction.

# Confusables

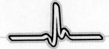

## allude/elude

**Allude** means to refer to something indirectly.

**Elude** means to hide from or escape.

---

 The robber managed to **elude** the police by racing away on a motorbike.

 The robber managed to **allude** the police by racing away on a motorbike.

---

 The MD **alluded** to the recent failed takeover attempt in his speech.

 The MD **eluded** to the recent failed takeover attempt in his speech.

# Confusables

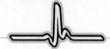

## bare/bear

**Bare** means uncovered or naked.

**Bear** means:
1. A large, dangerous, furry mammal.
2. To carry.
3. To have a tolerance for or endure.
4. To carry in the mind (e.g., **bear** a grudge).
5. To be accountable for (e.g., **bear** responsibility).
6. To have a tolerance for (e.g., couldn't **bear** the responsibility).

 Please **bear** with us while we remodel our store.

 Please **bare** with us while we remodel our store. (Unless you want your customers to strip off their clothes and watch you working naked!)

# Confusables

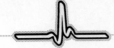

## bazaar/bizarre

A **bazaar** is a market, usually in the Middle East.

**Bizarre** means odd, unconventional, far-fetched.

 In that crazy costume, Kate's appearance was quite **bizarre**.

 In that crazy costume, Kate's appearance was quite **bazaar**.

 We went shopping in the **bazaar** and bought some gorgeous jewellery.

 We went shopping in the **bizarre** and bought some gorgeous jewellery.

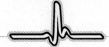

## berth/birth

A **berth** is:
1. A place for a ship or other vehicle to tie up or park.
2. A bunk on a ship.

A **birth** is the act of something being born.

 My cat gave **birth** to six cute kittens.

 My cat gave **berth** to six cute kittens.

 Jim managed to secure a **berth** on a boat heading for the West Indies.

 Jim managed to secure a **birth** on a boat heading for the West Indies.

# Confusables

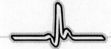

## biannual/biennial

**Biannual** means twice a year (same thing as semi-annual).

**Biennial** means every two years.

---

 We have a big **biannual** sales conference in January and July each year.

 We have a big **biennial** sales conference in January and July each year.

---

 The international competition takes place **biennially**, so we will have to wait until next year for our chance to win the gold trophy.

 The international competition takes place **biannually**, so we will have to wait until next year for our chance to win the gold trophy.

# Confusables

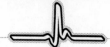

## border/boarder

A **border** is an edge around something,

A **boarder** is a person who stays in lodgings.

 There's an attractive **border** of flowers around the edge of the lawn.

 There's an attractive **boarder** of flowers around the edge of the lawn.

 The **boarders** get to play extra sports on the weekends.

 The **borders** get to play extra sports on the weekends.

# Confusables

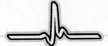

## cannon/canon

A **cannon** is a piece of artillery that fires cannonballs or water (and, occasionally, people).

A **canon** is a member of a religious order, or matters relating to religion.

 The ceremony was led by a **canon** from the nearby church.

 The ceremony was led by a **cannon** from the nearby church.

 The pirate ships were well stocked with powerful **cannons**.

 The pirate ships were well stocked with powerful **canons**.

# Confusables

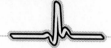

## canvas/canvass

**Canvas** is a surface for painting upon.

**Canvass** is a verb (a "doing" word) meaning to conduct a survey or to solicit votes or orders.

 A child's mind is a fresh **canvas** on which to paint a lifetime's knowledge.

 A child's mind is a fresh **canvass** on which to paint a lifetime's knowledge.

 Curly strolled through the canteen **canvassing** the students for their votes.

 Curly strolled through the canteen **canvasing** the students for their votes.

# Confusables

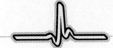

## capital/capitol

**Capital** can mean:
1. An accumulated sum of money, or the main stock or fund of a business.
2. Involving or affecting the head.
3. Most important or chief.
4. Punishable by death.
5. Uppercase letters.
6. A seat of government (usually a city).

 **Capitol** means a building in which a legislature meets.

 London is the **capital** of England.

 London is the **capitol** of England.

 The legislature opened its new session in the **capitol** today.

 The legislature opened its new session in the **capital** today.

 There are only a few states that currently support **capital** punishment.

 There are only a few states that currently support **capitol** punishment.

# Confusables

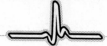

## chow/ciao

A **chow** is a large furry dog with a purple tongue or a slang word for food.

**Ciao** is an Italian greeting or farewell.

 As the friends parted, Mario called out a friendly "**Ciao**!" to Luigi.

 As the friends parted, Mario called out a friendly "**Chow**!" to Luigi.

# Confusables

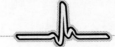

## cite/sight/site

**Cite** means to refer to something.

**Sight** means the ability to see.

**Site** means a location.

 I would like to **cite** the case of the missing armadillo.

 I would like to **sight** the case of the missing armadillo.

 Fred caught **sight** of the two lovers hiding in the stationery cupboard.

 Fred caught **site** of the two lovers hiding in the stationery cupboard.

 This is the **site** of the new office building.

 This is the **cite** of the new office building.

# Confusables

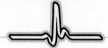

## climatic/climactic

**Climatic** refers to the climate.

**Climactic** refers to a climax.

 Global warming is causing **climatic** changes around the world.

 Global warming is causing **climactic** changes around the world.

 The movie rushed headlong towards an exciting, **climactic** finish.

 The movie rushed headlong towards an exciting, **climatic** finish.

# Confusables

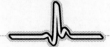

## coarse/course

**Coarse** means:
1. Rough.
2. Common, inferior, vulgar.
3. Consisting of large particles (e.g., **coarse** sand).

**Course** means:
1. The route or path taken by something that moves.
2. Movement of time (e.g., in the **course** of the year).
3. A mode of action or behaviour.
4. An orderly sequence of actions (e.g., a **course** of antibiotics or a course of studies).
5. A layer of building material (e.g., a **course** of red bricks).
6. Without any doubt (as used in "Of **course** ...").

---

 Of **course** you shall go to the ball!

 Of **coarse** you shall go to the ball!

---

 The cow's tongue felt like **coarse** sandpaper on the back of my hand.

 The cow's tongue felt like **course** sandpaper on the back of my hand.

# Confusables

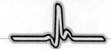

## complement/compliment

A **complement** is something that goes well with something else, e.g., complementary colours, or that completes something.

A **compliment**, on the other hand, is what you give to somebody when you say something nice to them. It can also mean something that you give away—e.g., complimentary tickets.

 This red wine is a perfect **complement** to the rare roast beef.

 This red wine is a perfect **compliment** to the rare roast beef.

 Mick tried to get back into Sue's good books by paying her **compliments**.

 Mick tried to get back into Sue's good books by paying her **complements**.

 Our clinic offers **complementary** therapies (therapies that work together).

 Our clinic offers **complimentary** therapies (unless you plan to give treatments away for free).

# Confusables

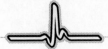

## council/counsel

**Council** is a noun (a "thing" word) meaning an administrative group.

**Counsel** is a verb (a "doing" word) that means to give advice, usually by somebody in authority. It's also a noun (a "thing" word) meaning advice.

 Joan was very pleased with herself for being elected to the town **council**.

 Joan was very pleased with herself for being elected to the town **counsel**.

 Fred sought the **counsel** of his tutor when he ran into difficulties with his studies.

 Fred sought the **council** of his tutor when he ran into difficulties with his studies.

# Confusables

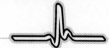

## curb/kerb

**Curb** is a verb (a "doing" word) meaning to cut short or curtail.

   It is also the edge of a path.

   A **kerb** is the edge of a path.

---

 Nick was advised to **curb** his appetite for beer at the annual company dinner.

 Nick was advised to **kerb** his appetite for beer at the annual company dinner.

---

---

 Be careful not to trip over the **kerb**.

 Be careful not to trip over the **curb**.

---

# Confusables

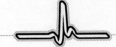

## desert/dessert

**Desert** means:

1. A dry, hot, sandy place.
2. A verb (a "doing" word) meaning to abandon.
3. What one deserves (as in "just deserts").

A **dessert** is something sweet that you eat after a meal.

 Try one of our delicious home-made **desserts**!

 Try one of our delicious home-made **deserts**!

 The group might have died in that **desert** if they hadn't found the oasis.

 The group might have died in that **dessert** if they hadn't found the oasis.

 The thief got his just **deserts** and was locked up for five years.

 The thief got his just **desserts** and was locked up for five years.

# Confusables

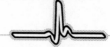

## device/devise

A **device** is a gadget or tool.

**Devise** is a verb (a "doing" word) that means to plan, contrive, form in the mind.

 The Super Widget is a great **device** for holding things in place.

 The Super Widget is a great **devise** for holding things in place.

 We need to **devise** a plan to get out of this mess.

 We need to **device** a plan to get out of this mess.

# Confusables

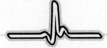

## discreet/discrete

**Discreet** means circumspect or judicious.

**Discrete** means separate, distinct, or unconnected.

 Let's be **discreet** about this embarrassing little problem.

 Let's be **discrete** about this embarrassing little problem.

 The Widget is made up of six **discrete** parts.

 The Widget is made up of six **discreet** parts.

# Confusables

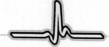

## dual/duel

**Dual** means *two of a kind* (such as **dual** titanium headlamps).

A **duel** is a fight (traditionally, with swords) between two people.

 All of our training vehicles feature **dual** controls for the instructor and student.

 All of our training vehicles feature **duel** controls for the instructor and student.

 The two knights agreed to a **duel** at dawn.

 The two knights agreed to a **dual** at dawn.

# Confusables

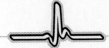

## dyeing/dying

You can change the colour of something by **dyeing** it.

The event of life expiring is known as **dying**.

 I'm **dying** to meet your mother.

 I'm **dyeing** to meet your mother.

 I'm **dyeing** my T-shirt bright blue.

 I'm **dying** my T-shirt bright blue.

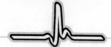

## emigrate/immigrate

If you move out of a country, you **emigrate** from it; but you **immigrate** into a new country.

 I'm going to **emigrate** to Australia.

 I'm going to **immigrate** to Australia.

The above example might appear a little contradictory, but it can be clarified if we expand on it a little, like this:

I'm going to **emigrate** from England and **immigrate** to Australia.

# Confusables

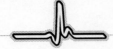

## eminent/imminent

**Eminent** means of high rank; towering or standing above others.

**Imminent** means about to happen.

 A change in the weather is **imminent**.

 A change in the weather is **eminent**.

# Confusables

## enquire/inquire

You're off the hook on this one—either version is acceptable!

# Confusables

## ensure/insure

**Ensure** means to make sure of something.

**Insure** means to purchase insurance.

 Please **ensure** that you fill in the forms correctly.

Please **insure** that you fill in the forms correctly.

# Confusables

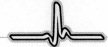

## formally/formerly

**Formally** means in a formal manner.

**Formerly** means on a previous occasion.

 **Formerly**, we used to leave early on Fridays.

 **Formally**, we used to leave early on Fridays.

# Confusables

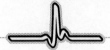

## gamble/gambol

**Gamble** means to bet money on a race, game of chance, or other activity.

**Gambol** means to prance around gleefully.

 Sue foolishly **gambled** all her money away.

 Sue foolishly **gambolled** all her money away.

 We watched the lambs **gambol** in the field.

 We watched the lambs **gamble** in the field.

# Confusables

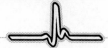

## hoard/horde

A **hoard** is a collection of valuables hidden away. It's also a verb (a "doing" word) meaning to accumulate things and store them away for future use.

A **horde** is a large group of people, usually threatening in some manner.

 My mother keeps a **hoard** of chocolate in her wardrobe.

 My mother keeps a **horde** of chocolate in her wardrobe.

 An angry **horde** of disgruntled workers was waiting for us at the factory gates.

 An angry **hoard** of disgruntled workers was waiting for us at the factory gates.

# Confusables

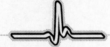

## holey/holy/wholly

**Holey** means having many holes.

**Holy** means belonging to, derived from, or associated with a divine power; sacred.

**Wholly** means completely.

 This Swiss cheese is very **holey**.

 This Swiss cheese is very **holy**.

 The wall was **wholly** covered with graffiti.

 The wall was **holy** covered with graffiti.

# Confusables

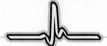

## its/it's

**Its** means belonging to it.

**It's** is a contraction of **it is** or **it has**.

 Place the bulb carefully into **its** holder.

 Place the bulb carefully into **it's** holder.

If you are unsure as to whether the apostrophe should or should not be there, you can use this simple test:

Expand the word **its** out into "it has" or "it is". If the sentence still makes sense, then the apostrophe belongs there; if it doesn't, then the apostrophe does not belong.

For example:
If you expand

>   *Remove the product carefully from **it's** packaging*

to:

>   *Remove the product carefully from **it is** packaging,*

this clearly doesn't make sense! So, the apostrophe does **not** belong here.

On the other hand …

If you expand

>   *I'm sure **it's** in here somewhere*

to:

>   *I'm sure **it is** in here somewhere,*

this makes perfect sense. So the apostrophe **does** belong this time.

Also see the Apostrophes topic in Section 1 for a more detailed discussion of the use of apostrophes.

# Confusables

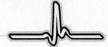

## leak/leek

A **leak** is an unwanted release of something (sometimes, information).

A **leek** is a vegetable particularly popular in Wales.

 There was gravy all over the table because of a **leak** in the serving dish.

 There was gravy all over the table because of a **leek** in the serving dish.

 A popular dish in Wales is **leek** and potato soup.

 A popular dish in Wales is **leak** and potato soup..

# Confusables

## licence/license

 These two are used interchangeably.

 **Licence** is a noun (a "thing" word) meaning a certificate giving permission (a marriage licence, for example).

**License** is a verb (a "doing" word) meaning to certify, give permission, authorise.

 You're supposed to have a **licence** for that dog.

 You're supposed to have a **license** for that dog.

 It costs over £100 per user to **license** the new software.

 It costs over £100 per user to **licence** the new software.

# Confusables

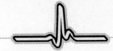

## lightening/lightning

**Lightening** means making something lighter (either in colour or weight).

**Lightning** is flashes of light in the sky during a thunderstorm.

---

 There was a fantastic display of **lightning** during last night's storm!

 There was a fantastic display of **lightening** during last night's storm!

---

 It was a great **lightening** of a load to get rid of that old house.

 It was a great **lightning** of a load to get rid of that old house.

---

# Confusables

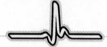

## loose/lose

**Loose** is the opposite of tight.

**Lose** means to part company with something in an unplanned manner.

 We mustn't **lose** sight of the goal.

 We mustn't **loose** sight of the goal.

 Don't let the dog **loose** in the park.

 Don't let the dog **lose** in the park.

# Confusables

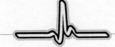

## moral/morale

**Moral** means:
1. Concerned with ethical behaviour.
2. A moral lesson.

**Morale** means mental attitude.

 **Morale** was high after the team won the first round.

 **Moral** was high after the team won the first round.

 The **moral** of the story is: Don't mess with the boss's daughter.

 The **morale** of the story is: Don't mess with the boss's daughter.

# Confusables

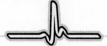

## now/know

Although these words don't actually sound the same, they are often confused, perhaps because the silent "k" is a bit mystifying.

**Now** means at the present time.

**Know** means to perceive; grasp in the mind with clarity or certainty.

 I don't **know** how to get to the new building from here.

 I don't **now** how to get to the new building from here.

# Confusables

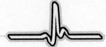

## of/off

**Of** means derived or coming from.

**Off** means the opposite of on.

 That car is veering way **off** course.

 That car is veering way **of** course.

 That's an interesting way **of** solving the puzzle.

 That's an interesting way **off** solving the puzzle.

# Confusables

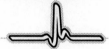

## palate/pallet/palette

A **palate** is the roof of the mouth, and is also used to refer to taste (as in, for example, "He has a delicate **palate**.")

A **pallet** is a portable platform for storing and transporting materials; also a small, hard, or makeshift bed.

A **palette** is a board on which artists mix their paints.

 That spicy curry isn't suited to my delicate **palate**.

 That spicy curry isn't suited to my delicate **palette**.

 Stack the magazines on that **pallet**, please.

 Stack the magazines on that **palette**, please.

 The artist's **palette** housed a rainbow of mixed colours.

 The artist's **palate** housed a rainbow of mixed colours.

# Confusables

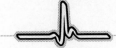

## pedal/peddle

A **pedal** is something you push with your foot (e.g., to make your bike go).

**Peddle** means to try to sell things (usually on the cheap).

 Mickey **pedalled** for all he was worth to try and win the race.

 Mickey **peddled** for all he was worth to try and win the race.

 I'll see if I can **peddle** these old phones at the flea market tomorrow.

 I'll see if I can **pedal** these old phones at the flea market tomorrow.

# Confusables

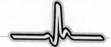

## personal/personnel

**Personal** means relating to an individual person.

**Personnel** are a group of people (usually, employees).

 Leave that alone—it's my **personal** property!

 Leave that alone—it's my **personnel** property!

# Confusables

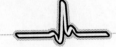

## pole/poll

A **pole** is:
1. A long rod.
2. The end of an axis, especially the Earth's (North **Pole**, South **Pole**).

A **poll** is:
1. A register of voters
2. The taking of a vote or public opinion by means of questioning

 We took a **poll** of the students' opinions on the new computer suite.

 We took a **pole** of the students' opinions on the new computer suite.

 Gemma still believes that Santa lives at the North **Pole**.

 Gemma still believes that Santa lives at the North **Poll**.

# Confusables

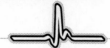

## pray/prey

To **pray** means to say a prayer.

**Prey** refers to an animal that is likely to end up as another animal's dinner. It's also a verb (a "doing" word) meaning *to hunt*.

 The owl swooped down on its **prey** with shocking speed in the darkness.

 The owl swooped down on its **pray** with shocking speed in the darkness.

 Let us all kneel down and **pray**.

 Let us all kneel down and **prey**.

# Confusables

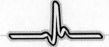

## principal/principle

**Principal** means the main or most important thing.

**Principle** has several meanings, but its most common use is to refer to the general rules of moral conduct.

 It's against my **principles** to wear a real fur coat.

 It's against my **principals** to wear a real fur coat.

 The **principal** cause of the breakdown was a small leak in the radiator.

 The **principle** cause of the breakdown was a small leak in the radiator.

# Confusables

## program/programme

These two are both acceptable, although generally **programme** is used to refer to a publication that lists events (such as a theatre programme).

 In the UK, **programme** is sometimes used to refer to a computer application (although it's considered to be a little old-fashioned these days).

# Confusables

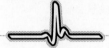

## rain/reign/rein

**Rain** is wet stuff that falls from the clouds.

**Reign** means to rule over (as a king or queen does).

A **rein** is a rope or leather strap used to control an animal, and it's also a verb (a "doing" word) meaning *to control*, as in *reining in one's emotions*.

 Use the **reins** to tell the horse which way you want to go.

 Use the **rains** to tell the horse which way you want to go.

 Queen Victoria set high moral standards during her **reign**.

 Queen Victoria set high moral standards during her **rein**.

# Confusables

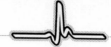

## role/roll

A **role** is a part that somebody plays.

A **roll** is a movement caused by repeatedly turning over and over on an axis.

 He was on a bit of a **roll** and couldn't seem to stop winning.

 He was on a bit of a **role** and couldn't seem to stop winning.

 Sanjiv was happy to take on the **role** of project manager.

 Sanjiv was happy to take on the **roll** of project manager.

# Confusables

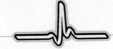

## sole/soul

**Sole** means only, or alone. It's also a type of fish.

Your **soul** is that part of you which thinks, feels, desires, etc. It's also a type of music.

 The little boy was the **sole** survivor of the shipwreck.

 The little boy was the **soul** survivor of the shipwreck.

 I really put my heart and **soul** into that performance!

 I really put my heart and **sole** into that performance!

# Confusables

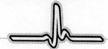

## stake/steak

A **stake** is:
1. A sharp, pointed stick.
2. Some money or other valuable that is offered up in a game of chance.

A **steak** is a thick slice of meat (usually beef).

 I'd **stake** my reputation on it.

 I'd **steak** my reputation on it.

 There's nothing I enjoy more than a thick, juicy fillet **steak**.

 There's nothing I enjoy more than a thick, juicy fillet **stake**.

# Confusables

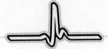

## stationary/stationery

**Stationary** means not moving.

**Stationery** is pens, paper, and other bits and pieces you might find in any office.

 Please go and get some pencils from the **stationery** cupboard.

 Please go and get some pencils from the **stationary** cupboard.

(Unless, of course, you are referring to the cupboard that doesn't move ...)

 The "joyrider" crashed into four **stationary** vehicles.

 The "joyrider" crashed into four **stationery** vehicles.

(Unless the four vehicles were delivery vans for an office supply company. Perhaps they were stationary stationery vehicles.)

# Confusables

## storey/story

**Storey** refers to a floor level in a building.

A **story** is a narrative, a tale.

 **Story** is acceptable for both meanings.

 We're moving to a new ten-**storey** office building.

 We're moving to a new ten-**story** office building.

 Karen made up quite a wild **story** to account for her tardiness.

 Karen made up quite a wild **storey** to account for her tardiness.

# Confusables

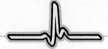

## suit/suite

A **suit** is:
1. A number of articles made to be worn together—e.g., a **suit** of armour, a business **suit**.
2. The process or act of suing.
3. A courtship.
4. A series or set.

A **suite** is:
1. A set of furniture or rooms.
2. A sequence of instrumental movements.

 I would hate for others to follow **suit**.

 I would hate for others to follow **suite**.

 Sale now on! Save 20% on our living room **suites**!

 Sale now on! Save 20% on our living room **suits**!

# Confusables

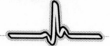

## taught/taut

**Taught** is the past tense of teach.

**Taut** means pulled tight.

 My dad **taught** me how to drive.

 My dad **taut** me how to drive.

 Pull the string **taut** to secure the package.

 Pull the string **taught** to secure the package.

# Confusables

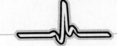

## there/their/they're

**There** means *in that place* or *in that respect*.

**Their** means *belonging to them*.

**They're** is a contraction of *they are*.

 Please let us know if **there** is any way that we can improve our service.

 Please let us know if **their** is any way that we can improve our service.

 Everybody can join in the fun and sing along to **their** favourite tracks.

 Everybody can join in the fun and sing along to **there** favourite tracks.

 **They're** going to move out into the country.

 **Their** going to move out into the country.

 **There** are fourteen bright colour schemes from which to choose.

 **They're** are fourteen bright colour schemes from which to choose.

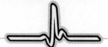

## til/till

**Til** is not actually a word. In its correct form (**'til**) it is an abbreviation for **until**.

**Till** means:
1. To work the soil.
2. A cash register.

**Till** is NOT an abbreviation for **until**!

 'Til death us do part.

 Till death us do part.

# Confusables

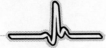

## to/too

**To** is a word that can have a number of meanings such as:
1. Towards or in the direction of (e.g., going **to** school)
2. As part of a verb (e.g., "Don't forget **to** close the door").

**Too** means as well as, in addition to, more than is required (e.g., "Don't be **too** long at the grocery store").

The easiest way to get this one right is simply to remember the meaning of **too**, and if that doesn't fit the sentence, then it must be **to**.

 This project is **too** complicated for me.

 This project is **to** complicated for me.

# Confusables

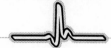

## told/tolled

**Told** is the past tense of tell (e.g., "I **told** you so!")

**Tolled** is the past tense of the verb toll, which means to sound, as a bell does, especially with slow, measured strokes.

 The church bell **tolled** to summon us to worship.

 The **tolling** of the bell **told** the people to come to the church.

 The church bell **told** to summon us to worship.

# Confusables

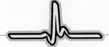

## trooper/trouper

A **trooper** is a soldier.

A **trouper** is a travelling entertainer.

 The **troupers** performed some amazing acrobatics.

 The **troopers** performed some amazing acrobatics.

 He's a real **trooper**!

 He's a real **trouper**!

 The **troopers** swarmed into the occupied village.

 The **troupers** swarmed into the occupied village.

# Confusables

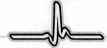

## tortuous/torturous

**Tortuous** means convoluted, or twisting and turning.

**Torturous** means extremely painful (as if one was being tortured).

 The team-building weekend was **torturous**!

 The team-building weekend was **tortuous**!

 The path wound **tortuously** through the forest.

 The path wound **torturously** through the forest.

# Confusables

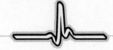

## weather/wether/whether

**Weather** refers to the atmospheric conditions around us—the rain, wind, sun, etc. It can also be used as a verb (a "doing" word) meaning to survive something.

A **wether** is a castrated ram.

**Whether** introduces the first part of two alternatives, such as "I don't know **whether** to go out or not". Often, the second part is left out and its meaning is assumed by the reader, for example, "I don't know **whether** to go out".

 Regardless of **whether** you like it or not, you're going to eat your vegetables.

 Regardless of **weather** you like it or not, you're going to eat your vegetables.

 Those poor **wethers** don't know what they're missing!

 Those poor **weathers** don't know what they're missing!

 Does anybody know what the **weather** will be like tomorrow?

 Does anybody know what the **whether** will be like tomorrow?

# Confusables

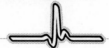

## who's/whose

**Who's** is a contraction (shortening) of **who is** or **who has.**

**Whose** denotes ownership of something.

 **Whose** letters are these?

 **Who's** letters are these?

 This is the man **who's** responsible for our new marketing campaign.

 This is the man **whose** responsible for our new marketing campaign.

 **Who's** ready for lunch?

 **Whose** ready for lunch?

 **Who's** got the latest stock report?

 **Whose** got the latest stock report?

An easy way to figure out which to use is to substitute **who is** or **who has** for the **whose** or **who's** in your sentence, and see if it still makes sense. If it does, then **who's** is correct; if it doesn't then you should use **whose**. For example, if you expand

> *I spoke to a friend **who's** business was in trouble*

to

> *I spoke to a friend **who is** business is in trouble,*

it doesn't make sense. So the correct choice in this case would be ***whose***.

# Confusables

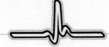

## yoke/yolk

A **yoke** is a wooden frame that joins things together, most often a pair of oxen or other animals.

A **yolk** is the yellow part of an egg.

 Try not to break the **yolk** when you crack the egg into the pan.

 Try not to break the **yoke** when you crack the egg into the pan.

# Confusables

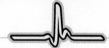

## your/you're

**Your** means *belonging to you*.

**You're** is a contraction of *you are*.

 Here are **your** instructions for today.

 Here are **you're** instructions for today.

 Surely **you're** not serious!

 Surely **your** not serious!

If you're unsure as to whether to include the apostrophe or not, try the following simple test:

Expand the word out into **you are** and see if the sentence still makes sense. If it does, then **you're** is correct; if it doesn't, then you should use **your**.

For example, if you expand
*Take **you're** hands off of that*
into:
*Take **you are** hands off of that,*
it doesn't make sense at all! So, the correct choice would **your**.

On the other hand …

If you expand
***You're** going to get into trouble over that*
into:
***You are** going to get into trouble over that,*
it makes perfect sense, so in this case the correct choice would be **you're**.

# Section 4

# *Points of Grammar*

We promised not to bog you down with technical terms, but if you want descriptions of the parts of grammar that we refer to in the rest of the book, you'll find them here.

# Points of Grammar

## Adjective

An adjective is a "describing word"—one that tells us something about a noun. Examples include:

| | |
|---|---|
| an **old** man | a **black** dog |
| a **pink** pig | a **sharp** sword |
| a **purple** Martian | a **noisy** train |

# Points of Grammar

## Adverb

An adverb adds meaning to or qualifies a verb, adjective, or another adverb—think of it as an "add-verb". They are usually formed by adding "ly" to the end of an adjective.

Qualifying a verb:

| | |
|---|---|
| running **quickly** | speaking **loudly** |
| go **quietly** | climb **carefully** |

Qualifying an adjective:

| | |
|---|---|
| **really** hot | **extremely** deep |
| **terribly** difficult | |

Qualifying another adverb:

| | |
|---|---|
| **very** quietly | **really** well |

# Points of Grammar

## Collective Noun

A collective noun is a single name for a group of things. For example "audience" is a collective noun for a group of people; "litter" is a collective noun for a group of puppies or kittens.

The important thing to remember about collective nouns is that they are usually treated as singular nouns when they are referred to in a sentence. For example:

> *The* litter *of kittens* **was** *born on Sunday*
as opposed to
> *The litter of kittens* **were** *born on Sunday.*

 The board of directors **has** decided to offer a new stock option.

 The board of directors **have** decided to offer a new stock option.

In some cases, however, it is appropriate to treat a collective noun as a plural—for example, when the group is considered as a group of individuals. In the following example, we are clearly referring to audience members as individuals:

> *The audience,* **who were** *clapping enthusiastically, were obviously enjoying* **themselves**.

If you are not sure as to whether a particular word is a collective noun or not, think about whether you would precede it with either "a" or "an" as opposed to "some". If you would, then it's a collective noun. For example, would you say "a herd of cows" or "some herd of cows"?

You would say "a herd of cows", so it is a collective noun.

*In the English TV series* Inspector Morse, *the protagonist asks his colleagues at the scene of a crime if there is a collective noun for a group of pathologists. They decide on "a body of pathologists".*

# Points of Grammar

## Noun

A noun is a "thing" word—a person, place, or object.

There are also specific types of noun:

### Abstract Noun
Feelings, qualities, events, states—things that have no physical existence are abstract nouns. Examples include: music; happiness; fun; advice; time.

### Collective Noun
A single name for a group (see the Collective Nouns topic on Page 180).

### Common Noun
A noun which is not the name of a specific person, place, or thing—the opposite of a **proper noun**.

### Mass Noun
A mass noun has no plural form, and is often thought of as a substance. They are uncountable things. Examples include: butter; smoke; gas; sugar; beer; sand.

### Proper Noun
A **specific** person, place, or thing, e.g., John Smith, The New York Times, Westminster Abbey, Lassie, Paris. Proper nouns are always uppercased. The opposite of a **common noun**.

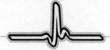

# Points of Grammar

## Sentence Structure—the Basics

There are three basic rules that should be obeyed for every sentence that you write:

1.  Every sentence must start with a capital letter.

 We are pleased to provide this additional service at no cost to you.

 we are pleased to provide this additional service at no cost to you.

### Exception to the rule:
If a word would normally *specifically* be in all lower case, so it should remain when it appears at the beginning of a sentence. For example:

*van Gogh may have been a bit odd, but he was a great artist.*

2.  Every sentence must end with a full stop (***period***, to Americans) or other punctuation such as a question mark or exclamation mark.

 Why have you sent this back to me?

 Why have you sent this back to me

3.  Every sentence must contain a verb ( a "doing" word).

A sentence can be very short—as short as one word—and still fill those three requirements:

*Go!*

Additionally, if a sentence is followed by another sentence in the same paragraph, it must be followed by a space. (Note: that's **one** space, not two!)

# Points of Grammar

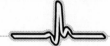

## Verb

A verb is a "doing" word. Every sentence must contain a verb in order to make sense.

A verb refers to an action—such as go, walk, sing, do, or a state—such as be or own.

One way to recognise a verb it to put "to" in front of it and see if it makes sense:

| | |
|---|---|
| *to go* | *to walk* |
| *to run* | *to be (or not to be)* |
| *to play* | *to act* |

Or to add "ing" to it:

| | |
|---|---|
| *going* | *walking* |
| *running* | *being* |
| *playing* | *acting* |

---

**More Info** This description is quite a simplistic one: there are a number of special types of verb. If you are interested in finding out more, an excellent source is www.usingenglish.com.

# Section 5

# *Further Reading*

Hungry for more information? You'll find some helpful suggestions on where to dig deeper in this section.

# Further Reading

## Books

*The Chicago Manual of Style*
Published by The University of Chicago Press, this hefty book (more than 900 pages) has become the essential reference for writers, editors, publishers, and other people who really care about the grammar and style of their published work. Currently (April 2004) in its 15th edition, the *CMS* (as it is affectionately known) is updated from time to time to reflect changes in modern style and usage.

*A Dictionary of Modern English Usage*
Many writers wouldn't put pen to paper (or pixels to computer screen) without having their copy of *Fowler's* (as this book is affectionately known) handy. First published in 1926, it has been periodically updated to keep it "modern". Original author: Henry Fowler.

*The Elements of Style*
Smaller than the Chicago or Oxford manuals, *The Elements of Style* has long been a favourite of students and writers. This little paperback will easily travel with you, but can still provide the answers to most grammar and punctuation questions. Often referred to as *Strunk & White's* after its original authors. Authors: William Strunk Jr., E. B. White, Roger Angell.

*The Oxford Dictionary of English Grammar*
Need to quickly find out what a mandative subjunctive is? This handy reference will answer such questions for you. It even includes an informative diagram of the human speech organs.

*The Oxford Style Manual*
Published by Oxford University Press, this is the British equivalent of the *Chicago Manual of Style*. Weighing in at more than 1,000 pages, it provides a detailed reference to grammar and usage from the British perspective.

# Further Reading

## Internet

Note: Thanks to the ever-changing nature of the Internet, we can't guarantee that these links will remain active! We suggest that you check the Grammar Cookbook web site (www.trackerpress.com/grammarbook) for an up-to-date list.

*www.apostrophe.fsnet.co.uk/*
This is the home of The Apostrophe Protection Society: a web site devoted to the correct use of the apostrophe. There's an amusing section showing pictures of apostrophe abuse, and a message and discussion forum. If you have any questions about apostrophe use, this is the place to look!

*ccc.commnet.edu/grammar/*
A comprehensive guide to grammar and punctuation, with helpful examples. There's a quiz and puzzle section that's educational and—yes—fun!

*www.acronymfinder.com*
"The world's most complete reference to acronyms, abbreviations, and initialisms." Need to find out what a WWWW is? Look it up on acronymfinder.com.

*www.grammarbook.com/*
A useful resource for looking up some specific grammar and punctuation rules. Also includes exercises and tests that you can use to practice getting it right.

*www.press.uchicago.edu/Misc/Chicago/cmosfaq/about.html*
This is the web site of *The Chicago Manual of Style*. If you use the CMS, you can use the **Search the Manual** facility to find references to topics in the book (note: it doesn't show you the topics—just where to find them in the book).

*www.usingenglish.com*
An excellent online source for finding answers to your grammatical queries. Want to know what a past participle is? Search the Glossary. There are a number of discussion forums, such as **Ask a Teacher** and **FAQ** to help you find the answers to those tricky grammar and style questions.

*www.ucl.ac.uk/internet-grammar/*
This is the home of The Internet Grammar of English—a free on-line grammar course. It's designed for university undergraduates, but anybody can use it.

# Section 6

# *Index*

# Index

# Index

# Index

# Index

# Index

We hope you have found this book helpful, and we would love to hear your feedback. Please send your comments to tgc@trackerpress.com.

Thank you!

## Other Books by Pat Bensky

*A Lizard in the Sun—*
*Three Years of Zero Budget Travels*

What would you do if you were desperate to travel around the world, but you had little or no money to finance your trip? You could stay home feeling sorry for yourself, keep putting it off until you could afford it, or just pack a bag and go, hoping to be able to live on your wits and find work along the way.

That's what Pat Bensky did in her early twenties, and it led to a three-year adventure as she worked her way around Europe, North Africa, the West Indies, Bahamas, and the USA. At times she was hungry, homeless, sick, miserable, ecstatic; was almost lost at sea, and cured of a serious illness by a West Indian witch doctor. But her resourcefulness, courage, and positive attitude steered her through the hard bits, and when she got to California, she decided that she'd found a place worth staying in.

*"... a guide book for today's youngsters considering setting off on similar jaunts."—Brian Page, British Mensa Magazine, Nov. 2003*

*"I've found it increasingly difficult to read books as I've got older. I used to devour them when I was at college, but I think that age has brought responsibility and deadlines and commitments and all those things that mean you can't sit down for an hour or more and just read. So recent years are full of books that never got past the second chapter. But you've written something that, once I started it, I just had to finish - I don't know how you managed that!"—David Hyde*

*"I read your book in one breath! It's amazing how brave and courageous you are! Couldn't stop reading to find out what was next."—Evelina Li*

*"I enjoyed your book. Ideal holiday reading. When is the next one coming out? I am sure you must have plenty more adventures for another one."—Jean Maskell*

*"I bought five copies of your book--planning to send them to my sisters and brother. It's great, a fast lively read."—Jude McGee*

*"It is a light funny and optimistic look at life travelling the globe by a person that has made a success of her life. This was against all the odds and with no money or parental help to do so. And shows you that there is good out there it's not all bad just be careful and enjoy your life while you have it. The book reads well I just could not put it down and read it from cover to cover and loved every second of it."—Paul Robinson*

See www.patbensky.com for more details, and pictures!

Lightning Source UK Ltd.
Milton Keynes UK
05 November 2010

162416UK00001B/12/A